CENTRAL PARK
NYC

In Memoriam

Charles Ryskamp

1926–2010

CENTRAL PARK
NYC

An Architectural View

ANDREW ZEGA AND BERND H. DAMS

New York · Paris · London · Milan

First published in the United States of America in 2013 by
RIZZOLI INTERNATIONAL PUBLICATIONS, INC.
300 Park Avenue South, New York, NY 10010
www.rizzoliusa.com

ISBN-13: 978-0-8478-4079-4
Library of Congress Control Number: 2013933280

Text and watercolor illustrations (unless otherwise noted):
© 2013 Edward Andrew Zega and Bernd H. Dams
www.architecturalwatercolors.com
Photography and additional illustrations credited individually throughout.

Distributed to the U.S. Trade by Random House, New York

Front cover: The Music Pavilion or Old Bandstand, authors' watercolor.
Back cover: Ramble Arch, photograph © 2013 Edward Andrew Zega.
Endpapers: Sculpture at Bethesda Terrace, photograph © 2013 Gwen Williams.

Designed by Andrew Zega

Printed and bound in China
2013 2014 2015 2016 2017 / 10 9 8 7 6 5 4 3 2 1

CONTENTS

PREFACE

*The city seen for the first time, in its first wild promise
of all the mystery and beauty in the world.*

F. Scott Fitzgerald, *The Great Gatsby*

Well over a decade ago now, we both lived in Manhattan, both a stone's throw from Central Park. One of us, then a junior editor at a major Midtown publisher, had the luxury of being able to walk to work by traversing Lilac Walk and skirting Sheep Meadow, leaving the park at Grand Army Plaza to reach Fifth Avenue. New York being New York, occasionally one encountered Woody Allen commuting crosstown on foot among the steady stream of morning joggers, dog walkers and sneaker-clad office workers. Central Park was our backyard; we bicycled the park drives on weekends, picnicked and sunbathed on Sheep Meadow in summer and set off on walks that had no destination in any season, simply for the pleasure of discovery.

Two late-night taxi routes are graven in memory as the apotheosis of life in Manhattan and have never lost their power to enthrall; one is riding uptown via Sixth Avenue and leaning back to watch the magnificent parade of Midtown skyscrapers unscroll against the luminous purple of the night sky; the other is traversing the park at 66th Street and turning to glimpse the illuminated wall of Central Park South silhouetted against the dark expanse of Sheep Meadow and the black scrim of foliage beyond. Unlike Byron, Shelley, Goethe or Ruskin, one needn't seek out earth's extremes to experience a modern incarnation of the Sublime; a late-night Manhattan taxi ride will more than do.

After completing three exhibitions on the subjects of French garden architecture and the architecture of Louis XIV, thematically intertwined projects that occupied us for over a decade, spawned two books and incidentally brought us to Paris, we believed we had achieved our goals in that area and began to consider subjects for a new exhibition. Naturally, we turned to Charles Ryskamp for advice. Charles had been patron of our first two exhibitions at Didier Aaron, Inc., which in part benefited The Frick Art Reference Library, for which he worked tirelessly. He also had authored the preface to *Pleasure Pavilions and Follies*, our first book, and we always sought his counsel when planning exhibitions. But he was first and foremost a friend of rare fidelity and generosity of spirit. Charles had a nearly unique ability to make the world a finer, richer place simply by being in his presence—a place of abundance and fascination. We've met only two others with this rare gift and it is certainly the reason for his remarkable life and career, but we've also rarely laughed so hard with anyone. He is sorely missed.

Alan Salz, director of Didier Aaron's Manhattan gallery, had suggested that we turn to Central Park, as the city would celebrate the park's sesquicentennial anniversary year in 2003, and Charles agreed, remarking that it made perfect sense that we prepare an exhibition on the park now that we had settled in Paris, just as we had prepared our first exhibition on French garden architecture while living in Manhattan. He also agreed

Preceding pages: A series of architectural details from Bethesda Terrace, the Waldo Hutchins Bench, Glade Arch and again, Bethesda Terrace. Authors' watercolors.

Opposite: The marker stone for the Artists' Gate at Sixth Avenue and Central Park South. In 1862, the park's entrances were named to honor the diverse occupations and character of city residents, though they were never so labeled. In 1999, gracefully chiseled marker stones were set into the park's boundary wall at these gates to fulfill that original intention. Authors' watercolor.

to act again as patron of the exhibition, which would again in part benefit The Frick Art Reference Library.

Despite the logistical difficulties involved—we could no longer simply stroll over to the park to examine an object that interested us or consult the important collections of archival materials residing in Manhattan at whim—we determined to create a series of watercolors celebrating the beauty and diversity of Central Park's architectural heritage. The exhibition, named simply Central Park and held at Didier Aaron in October of 2003, presented watercolors matching the diversity of its subject, depicting both landmarks and lesser-known objects dating from the park's inception to nearly the present day. Among them are a series of watercolors measuring well over a yard long or wide, which depict architectural elements and sculptural details at life size, including a section of ironwork of Vanderbilt Gate at Conservatory Garden (*pp. 90−91*), stone ornaments from Bethesda Terrace (*pp. 53, 64, 65, 68, 69*) and a detail of the USS *Maine* Monument (*pp. 178−179*). We deliberately chose these subjects for their inherent graphic power and rendered them at a scale more associated with contemporary painting than with watercolor, though one would otherwise know nothing of this looking at them reproduced in these pages.

The tragedy of September 11, 2001 traumatized the city and the nation and cast a somber shadow over the park's sesquicentennial celebrations. Eight more years would pass before our American publisher, Charles Miers, and our editor, David Morton, felt that the time was right to pursue the book on Central Park's architectural legacy that we had always intended to write. The watercolors from our 2003 exhibition, augmented by a large number of recent works, are the nucleus of this book, and we will focus our attention foremost upon them and hew closely to the stories they impel us to tell. We are extremely grateful to the numerous photographers who have generously allowed us to complement our watercolors with their work, particularly Cornelis Verwaal, who has provided a number of magnificent photographs. We have also paid special attention to the park's early history when selecting secondary illustrations, for paradoxically they offer the shock of the new, though most are well over a century old.

The full narrative history of Central Park has been detailed by numerous writers, as have the lives and careers of Frederick Law Olmsted and Calvert Vaux, and we do not intend this book to be encyclopædic in scope. As its subtitle suggests, it is a personal view and one focused primarily on our own abiding passion, the fortuitous intersection of architecture and gardens. We encourage interested readers to seek out the books listed in the bibliography for more complete information on aspects of the park's history that we are unable to offer here, constrained as we are by the scope of our subject and by our belief that this work should be copiously illustrated, since the story we wish to tell is above all a visual one.

ARTISTS' GATE

INTRODUCTION

*Who can measure the value, generation after generation, of
such provisions for recreation to the overwrought, much-
confined people of the great town that is to be?*

Frederick Law Olmsted

AFTER YEARS OF EDITORIALIZING, competing proposals and heated debate, legislation
authorizing the creation of a "central park" on 778 acres of central Manhattan
between Fifth and Eighth Avenues from 59th to 106th streets was passed by the
New York State legislature in 1853. The city took title to the land in 1856 and clearing
work began soon thereafter, supervised by a young jack-of-all-trades, a former sailor,
former gentleman farmer, failed publisher and struggling literary man named Frederick
Law Olmsted. However, the design of the new park provided by his superior, surveyor
and military engineer Captain Egbert L. Viele, was (as Clarence Cook, a critic for the
New York Times, later remarked) "commonplace and tasteless," and an idealistic and
well-placed English-born architect, Calvert Vaux, former partner of the recently drowned
Andrew Jackson Downing, the renowned horticulturist, garden designer and essayist,
convinced the park's board of commissioners that the design be put to open competition.
Vaux later recalled, "Being thoroughly disgusted with the manifest defects of Viele's plan,
I pointed out whenever I had a chance, that it would be a disgrace to the City and to
the memory of Mr. Downing." Quick with a sense of great opportunity, Vaux sought out
Olmsted, who knew both the art of planting and the site's topography, and convinced
him to work in partnership on a design, submitted to a janitor late on the day of the
competition's close, March 31, 1858.

The Greensward plan they conceived, clearly superior to the other thirty-two entries,
was selected for execution. Their design, in the tradition of the naturalistic English landscape park, transformed the hardscrabble center of Manhattan Island into a scenic work
of art: rough-and-tumble shantytowns and bleak vistas of swamps, tangled underbrush
and rocky outcrops were systematically rebuilt in a monumental construction program
that would require over two decades to complete. Olmsted and Vaux envisaged a pastoral
landscape of intimate dells and copses that gave way to placid lakes and great open pastures,
the whole interlaced with independent pedestrian walks and carriage drives that ensured
easy access and unimpeded circulation. Their concern for public access and accommodation ensured that Central Park became the "People's Park" championed by Andrew Jackson
Downing, whose impassioned editorials had been instrumental in rallying support for the
park's creation.

In consequence, Central Park became the foremost urban landscape park in America,
a model and source of pride for a young nation, famed for its naturalistic design and the
beauty and harmony of its landscape features. These "natural" vistas were complemented
by an equally varied body of architecture. Together the sum of these works, including the
park's famed bridges and its diverse buildings—soon augmented by its sculpture and
monuments—was conceived primarily by Vaux, assisted by Jacob Wrey Mould, as crucial

*Opposite: Bethesda Terrace
and Fountain, Central Park's
architectural centerpiece and
Calvert Vaux's masterpiece.
Photograph by Cornelis Verwaal.*

in contributing to the park's function and beauty, and with time it has been recognized as an indispensable element of New York's cultural heritage and has been hailed as a profoundly influential artistic achievement.

"The great town that is to be"

Opposite: The aptly named Majestic Apartments at Central Park West and 72nd Street, perhaps the most photogenic of all buildings bordering Central Park. Photograph by Ed Yourdon.

Above: Boaters on the Lake near the rocky promontory of Hernshead. This view looks south toward Columbus Circle, with Central Park West's famed twin-spired apartments as a backdrop. The art deco Century is at center and the Majestic Apartments are at right. Photograph by Andrew Zega.

As is so oft noted, by the mid-nineteenth century America had already adopted, in journalist John L. O'Sullivan's words, a "manifest destiny to overspread [...] the continent." New York City was equally ambitious: In 1811—when Greenwich Village was indeed still a village—the city's commissioners had already projected Manhattan's street grid across isolated villages, farmland, work yards, swamps and hardscrabble wilderness to the island's northern tip (*pp. 22–23*). By mid century, its elites were debating the creation of a park nearly as large as the city itself, to be built on largely vacant land reached by country roads. Objective reality, captured in contemporary photographs, documents rough-and-tumble scrubland (*p. 28, top*), yet prime lots were already subject to speculation. Manhattan existed first and foremost in the mind; it was then built to fulfill that vision.

Likewise, Central Park was conceived as a verdant oasis, a refuge from a city that simply did not yet exist. In truth, the park's plan was the response to a collective vision, for even when completed (and for decades after), the park was largely bordered by nothing. A small enclave and a handful of shanties were razed, and a few hundred cows and sheep

15

were displaced to clear 1.3 square miles at the heart of Manhattan Island. Ultimately, the story of Central Park is the story of the frontier closing. It was plain to all that the Industrial Revolution was rapidly transforming New York and that the pace would only accelerate in the future. The city's leaders, who had made their fortunes exploiting its headlong growth, could already foresee Manhattan Island transformed into a metropolis of several million. By mid century, Downing was already decrying "this wanton desert of business and dissipation." In 1868, Cook wrote:

> The change that deprived New York of this rural character came not by slow and easily traced degrees, but suddenly ... too suddenly for the city's good. It was not growth, it was revolution, and provision had to be made so speedily for the population that began to pour in about 1830 ... that many things had to be done carelessly, many irretrievable blunders were committed.

The men who established Central Park understood this as fact and grasped the urgency of the park project and acted with newfound boldness and breadth of vision, assuming responsibility and stewardship for generations yet unborn. To the city's and the country's great good fortune, they were more than equal to their task. Central Park was revolutionary in ambition, scale and innovation, and its example would foster a parks movement that would profoundly alter the development of America's burgeoning cities, then extend to encompass the nation's natural treasures, to the inestimable benefit of all. It is a singular achievement and a splendid legacy.

Above: This panoramic view looking north from Midtown Manhattan encompasses the west side of Central Park with Sheep Meadow and the Lake in the foreground; the Great Lawn and the Reservoir appear at right in the middle distance. Photograph by Mathew Knott.

Opposite: Olmsted and Vaux densely planted the park's borders to create a buffer to the surrounding city. A view along Central Park South looking east, with the spire of the Sherry-Netherland Hotel silhouetted against a troubled summer sky. Photograph by Joseph O. Holmes.

Following pages: A projected view of Central Park engraved in 1859, "looking south from the Observatory," ultimately completed in 1871 as Belvedere Castle. In reality, the city's northern outskirts were then over a mile distant.

I

"THE PEOPLE'S PARK"

*Plant spacious parks in your cities, and unloose their gates
as wide as the gates of morning to the whole people.*

Andrew Jackson Downing, "The New-York Park," 1851

THERE IS NO PROFIT TO BE HAD in again retelling the history of Central Park in such limited space and after so many and expert retellings. Instead, we will here look at the park and its history through the prism of architecture and design, and when examining that architecture we will attempt to place it in its historical context and explain its social relevance. Like a prism, the chapters that follow divide the park into its constituent elements and offer us the opportunity to explain the ideas animating and underpinning the expression of those elements. In short, though a great deal of historical information will be presented, we are not interested in compiling an encyclopædia or in recounting history as a story; we will above all discuss the ideas, intentions, clashes and decisions that animated the men who made Central Park, and we hope to do so with a

Above: Calvert Vaux, the English-born architect, was brought to New York as a young man by Andrew Jackson Downing, who sought a partner to expand his flourishing business as a landscape designer. After Downing drowned in 1852, Vaux carried on his work and designed both the Bank of New York offices and a Manhattan residence for John A. C. Gray, a wealthy banker named to the first board of commissioners of Central Park. Gray facilitated rejection of Egbert Viele's initial park plan and the adoption of Vaux's recommendation that an open competition be held, and he championed Olmsted and Vaux's ultimate triumph.

Above: After a youth spent in a variety of colorful but failed ventures, Frederick Law Olmsted was named supervisor of Central Park in 1857 and worked under Viele's orders clearing obstructions, draining swamps and blasting and leveling the site in preparation for construction. Vaux sought him out and convinced him to form a partnership and prepare a joint design for the park that would be in direct competition with Viele's own. After receiving Viele's gruff assent, Olmsted and Vaux developed the Greensward plan that would guide Central Park's creation and launch Olmsted's storied career as America's seminal landscape architect.

fresh viewpoint, without resorting either to hagiography or cant. That being said, let us begin by examining the ideas, the passions and the world that gave birth to Central Park.

Pride and Prejudice

After immersing oneself in the painfully congealed circumlocutions and pedantic structurations of mid-nineteenth-century American prose, one is above all struck by the pervasive substrate of insecurity and the disturbing degree of self-awareness that this language embodies. Writers in the Victorian age were implacably scrupulous in ensuring that they left no nuance unenslaved—their guarded expression, in an age of conformity and anxiety, doubtless born of a universal fear of ridicule. Among all contemporaries, only Andrew Jackson Downing crafted texts of brevity, spirit and wit, thereby explaining his enormous popularity among his contemporaries.

The psychological portrait these texts delineate is, frankly, a Freudian playground: "Our democratic values" and "our democratic institutions" are relentlessly invoked to redress a profound inferiority complex. The simple fact that democracy exists in the United States is considered a miraculous and cathartic absolution and serves as a fiercely implemented defense against the lurking imputation of barbarism. English novelist

21

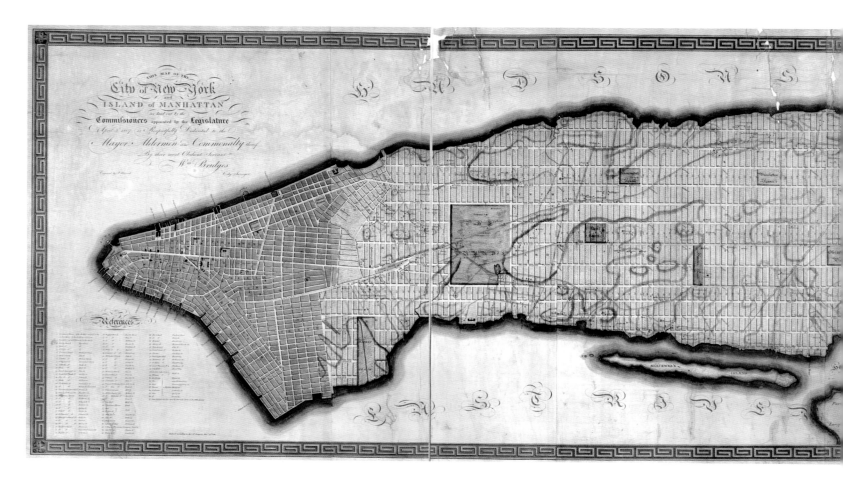

Anthony Trollope, visiting New York in 1862, pointedly captured this implacable and peculiarly American need for praise:

> The first question asked of you is whether you have seen the Central Park, and the second is as to what you think of it. It does not do to say simply that it is fine, grand, beautiful, and miraculous. You must swear by cock and pie that it is more fine, more grand, more beautiful, more miraculous than anything else of the kind anywhere. Here you encounter in its most annoying form that necessity for eulogium which presses you everywhere.

The screw then turns. After prophylactic protestations of impeccable political equality, American writers then revel in self-flagellation by way of comparisons to Europe, repeatedly throwing themselves on the balance and invariably finding themselves wanting. In England, French flour is prized and American flour "is the poorest on the market"; the former is whiter and finer and in all ways superior, reports a young Olmsted; European parks are extensive, magnificent and open to all while, in Downing's words—which echo the sentiments of Olmsted, Vaux, William Cullen Bryant, Mayor A. C. Kingsland and a host of lesser lights militating for a large public park—"deluded New-York has, until lately, contented itself with the little door-yards of space—mere grass-plots of verdure—which

Above: The famed Commissioners' Plan of 1811, which established Manhattan's orthogonal street grid. The disposition of avenues was determined by Middle Road (the future Fifth Avenue), surveyed in 1785 to access tracts sold by the city on and near the site of the future park. Of the nine projected small parks scattered about the grid, only Union and Manhattan squares were ultimately retained.

Opposite: The bustling port city of New York in 1857, on the eve of the construction of Central Park. Urbanization has reached to Murray Hill. Lithograph by Charles Parsons for Nathaniel Currier.

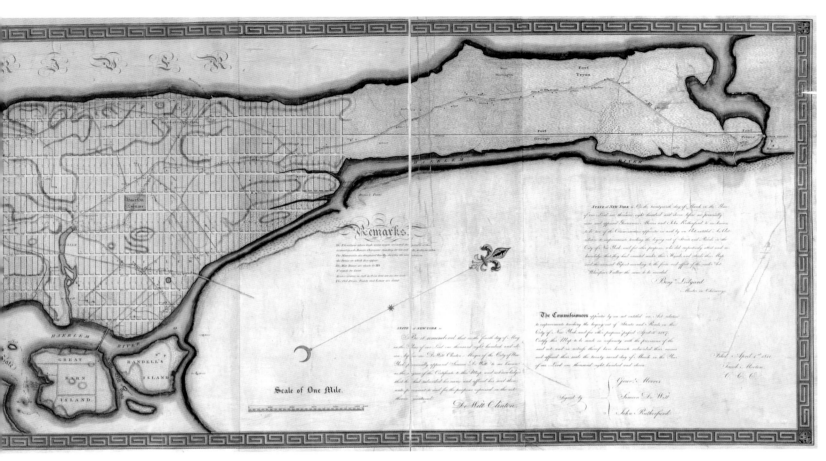

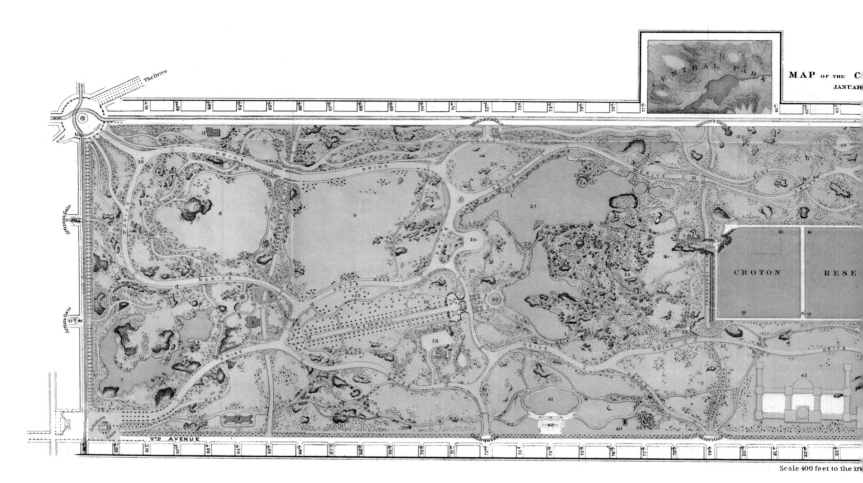

form the squares of the city, in the mistaken idea that they are parks.... Even the smaller [European] towns are provided with parks that would beggar the imagination."

To be sure, the United States was a youthful and politically volatile country beset by class and racial tensions, uneasy assimilation of immigrants and an increasingly disquieting north/south divide, and so such rhetoric is entirely understandable. The Constitution had been signed a mere seventy years prior to the competition for Central Park, and most mature Americans, including Olmsted, could recall the deaths of founders Thomas Jefferson and John Adams on July 4, 1826. Nonetheless, we are reminded, Americans are fiercely democratic—though the upper classes despise the lower, both despise immigrants and the poor, and everyone is loathe to socialize below their own station, making the very idea of a large public park problematic. An editorial published in the *New York Herald* expressed just such sentiments while the park was under construction:

> It is all folly to expect in this country to have parks like those in old aristocratic countries. When we open a public park Sam will air himself in it.... He will knock down any better dressed man who remonstrates with him. He will talk and sing, and fill his share of the bench, and flirt with the nursery-maids in his own coarse way. Now we ask what chance have William B. Astor and Edward Everett against this fellow-citizen of theirs? Can they and he enjoy the same place? Is it not

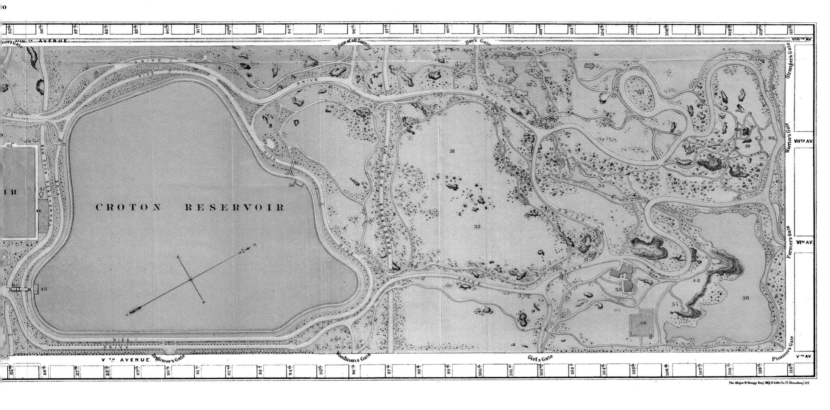

obvious that he will turn them out, and that the great Central Park will be nothing but a great bear-garden for the lowest denizens of the city?

Downing, clear-headed and sharp-witted, mocked this bigoted hypocrisy, believing the reverse was true and that public parks provided an important acculturating function:

Above: The map of Central Park in 1870. Major features that have subsequently changed are the removal of the rectangular old Croton Reservoir and the creation of the Great Lawn and Turtle Pond on the site and the suppression of the drive paralleling the Mall to its west. Also notable is Calvert Vaux's early plan for the "Art Museum" which would become the Metropolitan Museum of Art, found beneath the old reservoir. Though the Met's collections were then housed in a row house, the project rivals the scale of today's museum, the result of more than a century of expansion.

It is in fact not a little remarkable that, ultra democratic as are the political tendencies of America, its most intelligent social tendencies are almost wholly in a contrary direction.... It is, indeed, both curious and amusing to see the stand taken on the one hand by the million, that the park is made for "the upper ten," who ride in fine carriages, and, on the other hand, by the wealthy and refined, that a park in this country will be "usurped by rowdies and low people...." They can never have seen, how all over France and Germany, the whole population of the cities pass their afternoons and evenings together ... how the highest and the lowest partake alike of the common enjoyment.

The foremost reason for the park, in the eyes of the gentlemen driving the project forward, was to establish New York's bona fides as a major metropolis, and this explains the repeated comparisons made to London and the splendid example of Hyde Park.

The justifications that clothed this ambition were many and diverse—recreation, health, acculturation—but ultimately subsidiary. As the 1857 resolution crafted by John A. C. Gray, park commissioner and trustee of the Bank of New York, stated:

Above: Proposed alterations to Wembly park in Middlesex from Humphry Repton's Sketches and Hints on Landscape Gardening, *1794. Successor to William Kent and Lancelot "Capability" Brown, Repton was the last great English landscape designer of the eighteenth century and was highly influential among nineteenth-century designers.*

> ... being more than twice as large as Hyde Park in London—larger than Hyde Park and Kensington Gardens together—this Park complete, with its drives, walks, lawns, its groves, its fountains, and statuary, will constitute an unsurpassed feature of attraction to this city; and ... add the crowning feature to the attractions of this metropolis, and demonstrate that a people governing themselves not only admit of, but are satisfied with, nothing less than the highest expressions of art, as but developing the simplest and purest manifestations of nature.

A great deal has been written about the idealism and social conscience of the park's designers, particularly Olmsted's belief in the "restorative" effect of an ample, accessible pastoral landscape. However, its dark reverse was a paternalistic sexism concerning actual use of the park: gentlemen and boys were to pursue "manly" or "masculine pursuits" such as horseback riding, ball-playing and physical exercise, whilst the fairer sex was to tend to their offspring and take in the healthy air and the restorative powers of the peaceable scenery. Olmsted remarked in 1870, "The civilized woman is above all things a tidy woman. She enjoys being surrounded by bright and gay things perhaps not less than the savage, but she shrinks from draggling, smirching, fouling things and 'things out of keeping' more." The practical consequence of this mentality was that women were segregated and chaperoned by the park's very design, with a Ladies' Pond, a Ladies' Refreshment Salon and a Ladies' Pavilion all provided for their protection and sequestration.

Opposite, above: White Mountain Scenery, Franconia Notch, New Hampshire *by Asher B. Durand, 1857. The bucolic scenes crafted by the painters of the Hudson River School were deeply influential in mid-nineteenth-century America and reinforced the pastoral æsthetic of the English landscape park.*

Opposite, below: A detail of Vaux's pencil drawing of the "effect proposed" for the area that would become the playing fields; evocative sketches depicting the site's transformation were an integral part of the Greensward submission. This festive viewing pavilion was to be erected upon a stone outcrop later dubbed Umpire Rock but was never built.

The Quicksands of Ideology

In 1865, Vaux averred that Bethesda Terrace was "essentially Republican in its inspiration and general conception"—a remarkable assertion, considering that he had clearly modeled the structure upon the Sun King's vast Orangerie at Versailles (*p. 56*). Curiously, this patently false avowal, as well as the source of Bethesda Terrace's inspiration, have remained unexamined for over a century and a half, doubtless due to Vaux's flattering appeal to American exceptionalism. Though in this particular instance the gap between

Above: Before. One of Mathew Brady's 1857 views of the park site, looking north toward Vista Rock, crowned by the Receiving Reservoir's fire tower. Brady's photographs were provided to participants in the park's design competition.

Left: After. Cleverly, Vaux executed sketches reprising Brady's views, rendering the "effect proposed" based on the Greensward plan. Here, the Lake, the Ramble and an early version of the Belvedere transform Brady's bleak vista. The festive boating pavilion at left was not built but did apparently inspire a minor rustic gazebo (p. 139).

Right: John Singer Sargent's 1895 oil portrait of an aged Frederick Law Olmsted, commissioned by George Vanderbilt and painted at Biltmore, his palatial estate in Asheville, North Carolina, for which Olmsted designed the landscape.

Above: Bethesda Terrace under construction, looking northwest toward a rural Upper West Side. "View of the Terrace and Part of the Lake," photographed October 15, 1862, by Victor Prevost.

Left: The men who built Central Park, photographed on Willowdell Arch, which carries East Drive over a footpath near 67th Street. From left: comptroller Andrew H. Green, engineer George E. Waring, architect Calvert Vaux, gardener Ignaz Pilat, designer Jacob Wrey Mould and landscape architect Frederick Law Olmsted. Photograph by Victor Prevost, 1862.

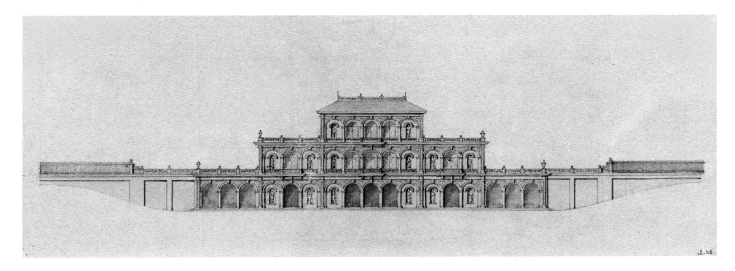

Above: The Garden Arcade was designed by Vaux and Mould as part of the original Greensward submission. The three-tiered pavilion, evoking an orangery, was intended to overlook a large, octagonally planned formal garden proposed for the site of today's Conservatory Water near Fifth Avenue at 75th Street; however, neither garden nor pavilion were executed.

source and rhetoric is more a chasm, Vaux's ingratiating oratorical legerdemain was a political necessity; how otherwise to justify the construction of an extremely costly and admittedly "not absolutely necessary" garden folly, let alone one modeled on one of the foremost symbols of France's Absolutist monarchy?

More broadly, Olmsted and Vaux did a truly remarkable job convincing most of their peers and the public that the garden æsthetics of the eighteenth-century English aristocracy incarnated "republican" ideals and were the best choice to guide the design of Central Park, and they were able to do so with such conviction because they had convinced themselves that informal plantings were somehow morally superior and even more salutary than formal ones. Viewed in opposition to the geometrical rigor of Le Nôtre's great works in late seventeenth-century France or even the contrived Vauxhall exoticism of the Anglo-Chinese folly garden that closed the eighteenth, the pastoral English landscape park crafted by Bridgeman, Kent, Brown and Repton over the course of the eighteenth century could fairly be said to be liberal in that it did not so overtly attempt to subjugate nature as these other schools had; that is, it is indeed superior if subtlety and sleight of hand are to be counted as virtues.

In truth, Olmsted, Vaux and their audience and judges had the choice of a single, massively popular style—one which had informed Romanticism, underpinned the potent Hudson River School movement and dominated Western garden theory and practice for over a century. The long-exhausted legacy of Le Nôtre was at the perigee of outdatedness and the Anglo-Chinese folly garden had simply been a passing fad that had long since passed; thus no style seriously challenged the hegemony of the English pastoral æsthetic. Even Captain Egbert L. Viele, the military engineer whose original plan for the park was so utterly graceless that Vaux effortlessly convinced the freshly constituted board of commissioners to put it aside and institute a competition, would resubmit his design, unrevised, with a written statement noting that "the greatest art is to conceal art," though he had created no art worthy to conceal.

Despite the intent of later critics to create drama where none existed, the pastoral vocabulary of the English landscape park hardly demanded the rousing campaign of

advocacy so often attributed to Olmsted and Vaux. In their written description of the Greensward submission, they never deemed it necessary to address the question of style at all except when it deviated from the accepted norm, as at the Promenade, later named the Mall, "an essential feature of a metropolitan park," where they explained that the requisite "grandeur and magnificence" could only be contrived by means of formal arrangement.

If anyone, outlying commissioners Robert Dillon and August Belmont, both financiers and Democrats and both cast as antagonists in the Central Park drama, were the ones in the true æsthetic vanguard. Both militated for a formal plan, and Dillon specifically proposed the separation of drives, footpaths and rides that became the park's guiding circulation principle, as well as an extensive bridle path "to accommodate manly and invigorating horsemanship" and even a suspension bridge linking Bethesda Terrace to the Belvedere. Though viewed today as heretics, they anticipated by decades the Beaux-Arts formalism of the City Beautiful movement and its apotheosis, the celebrated "White City" of the World's Columbian Exposition held in Chicago in 1893. (By then an éminence grise, Olmsted and his firm were named consulting landscape architects to the fair, and he selected the lakeside site, though architect John Root of Burnham & Root limned the Beaux-Arts master plan in a bravura performance while Olmsted looked on.) Likewise, Dillon's proposal for erecting a suspension bridge in the park was hardly the absurdity it appears on first glance but rather embodied his intention that the park showcase avant-garde technologies.

Opposite, above: The developer's dream—the projected Dakota Apartments and West Drive in 1891. Though the wealthy enjoyed carriage display in the park, it had "failed as a device for attracting fashionable residence," reported a real-estate guide in 1878.

Opposite, below: The reality. The newly completed Dakota and its neighbors, circa 1894.

Above: Home of the 400. Fifth Avenue saw rapid development below 72nd Street in the 1870s and was soon dubbed Millionaires' Row. Its epicenter was the Astor residence at 840 Fifth Avenue, a Loire Valley château designed by Richard Morris Hunt and completed in 1895.

Having traversed the Romantic age, the English landscape park has been duly romanticized and the unpleasant social and economic aspects of its historical roots forgotten. These extensive pleasure grounds may have been born in the Enlightenment, but they were conceived as purely aristocratic diversions that were harshly criticized by contemporaries as both decadent and socially predatory. Many parks owe their existence to the controversial and often violent practice of enclosure, a process whereby the aristocracy claimed control over domains of immense extent and privatized tracts of formerly common lands, sequestering them behind walls and evicting tenant farmers—and often the populations of entire villages—from settlements they had lived upon and worked for centuries. At enormous expense and using capital which formerly would have been invested in productive improvements, these lands were walled off, depopulated and given over to peacocks, swans and herds of exotic deer—all for the exclusive delectation of the privileged few.

The dark irony unrecognized by the park's designers and champions was that, ultimately, Central Park was a copy of an aristocratic pleasure ground built by and for immigrants and their descendants who had been impoverished and dispossessed from their ancestral lands by aristocrats who wished to construct private pleasure grounds. On the one hand, Central Park's philosophy and æsthetics are grounded in the anti-urban writings of Rousseau, which ennobled the "savage" in unconscious harmony with nature and sought respite from the deleterious effects of modernity and urbanity by seeking communion with nature, and on the other, by the English tradition of the landscape park, an artful

Opposite: The wealthy flocked to the park's drives with alacrity to display their finery and splendid carriages. Olmsted and Vaux ensured that footpaths paralleled the drives "so that pedestrians may have ample opportunity to look at the equipages and their inmates." For a small fee, children could also promenade the Mall in fine carriages pulled by goats.

Above: Maurice Prendergast's watercolors of city life and Central Park teem with the vibrant colors of the human parade. Central Park, New York (1901), Williams College Museum of Art.

Right: Prendergast's animated watercolor of Bethesda Terrace seen from the lower esplanade. The Mall, Central Park (1901), The Art Institute of Chicago.

refashioning of the land to conform to an Arcadian ideal depicted in the landscapes of Claude Lorrain, Nicolas Poussin and Salvator Rosa. Olmsted and Vaux linked this pastoral vision to democratic ideals to justify employing it as the basis for their æsthetic choice, though if one were to canvass the populations uprooted to craft these exquisite simulacra of rural nature, one would be hard-pressed to find a single dispossessed peasant who would confirm the thesis that proximity to Nature ennobled the spirit.

Nonetheless, Olmsted's oft-expressed belief in the redemptive and "restorative" effects of the pastoral landscape were profoundly held and entirely sincere, as was Vaux's conviction in the inspiring and elevating potential of beautiful and artistic creations. However, both men derived these worldviews from aristocratic traditions, but to their great credit they argued eloquently that such values were not exclusive to ruling elites but were indeed universal. Though at moments they stubbornly defended their artistic vision even to their own detriment, they were also practical men and acutely aware that the vast project they had embarked upon was a political and social undertaking well before it was an artistic one, and thus it demanded inspirational and aspirational justifications commensurate with its scale and cost.

Posterity owes both men an enormous debt of gratitude, but we should be aware that history-making—and history makers—always have an agenda, and history when first laid down is foremost an exercise in mythmaking, the art of weaving a tapestry of chosen facts and selected events into a seamless narrative to further a given ideology. And what is excluded is as important in crafting history as what is advanced as pertinent, and we should treat as suspect any history that aims to flatter us too eagerly.

Above: A tale of two cities. In the depths of the Great Depression, a Hooverville sprang up on the site of the old Receiving Reservoir (pp. 18–19), which Robert Moses had ordered demolished in 1929, to be replaced by the Great Lawn and Turtle Pond. This remarkable view looks east at the level of 80th Street; the obelisk (pp. 170–177) and the Metropolitan Museum of Art are seen at left.

Opposite: Grand Army Plaza from the north shore of the Pond, circa 1930. The magnificent urban ensemble of the Sherry-Netherland, Savoy Plaza and Plaza hotels was despoiled by the destruction of McKim, Mead & White's Savoy Plaza Hotel, razed in 1964 to permit construction of the GM Building.

THE MALL

A young man said to me, "I'm twenty-five; in the olden times one was famous at twenty-five." I said: "Yes, but in the olden times there were only about ten people, so of course they were all famous."

Nancy Mitford, *A Talent to Annoy*

ONE OF THE CHIEF ADVANTAGES of having been born in a prior century was that it was much easier to rise to prominence. Had not the steamer *Henry Clay* exploded in 1852, drowning Andrew Jackson Downing in the Hudson River, Frederick Law Olmsted would almost certainly be a mere footnote to history and Central Park would doubtless have been Downing's creation, seconded by Vaux. History was moving inevitably toward this end, but fate was rudely thwarted, and here Nancy Mitford's wry dictum comes to the fore. There was no heir apparent, no rival, no one at all who could easily step into Downing's role. Vaux, as Downing's surviving junior partner, understood this implicitly and to his great credit seized the opportunity he saw before him and politicked to establish an open competition for Central Park's design, giving new impetus to a project that was foundering aimlessly, its board members consumed by voting resolutions defining their own duties while the design of the park languished. Vaux was confident that the prize was his for the taking and astute enough to know that there simply was a dearth of professional landscaping talent to be had: No one else on the North American continent in 1857 was capable of submitting a compelling design for Central Park.

The remarkable thing in all this is not that Vaux and Olmsted won the competition to design Central Park—that was a foregone conclusion—but rather that their entry was so impressively accomplished. The two men—to what share and to what degree remains conjectural, but surely at the outset the question was weighted heavily in Vaux's favor—were well-versed in the English school of landscape and park design. The Greensward plan reveals not only conversancy with and command of the style's underlying principles, but more importantly it exhibits passages of true mastery and innovation surpassing mere synthesis, and the robust American hybrid the pair pioneered would reinvigorate the school and provide the impetus to carry it along for decades into the future. One can attest that Olmsted and Vaux transformed the English landscape park into a truly American idiom and that Central Park set the stage for and underpinned the great flowering of American urban planning and landscape design that was not long to follow.

"O great Poussin! O Nature's darling, Claude! Salvator!"
The fundamental precept underlying the design of the English landscape park—indeed the entirety of landscape architecture as practiced in the eighteenth and early nineteenth centuries—was the understanding that the garden designer assumed a nearly godlike role both in refashioning the land and in guiding the visitor through his creation along a predetermined circuit composed of a series of carefully constructed tableaux. The park or garden was literally a *tableau vivant*, or more precisely a linked series of living pictures, and the designer approached its composition as if he were an artist creating a landscape

Preceding page: Jacob Wrey Mould famously remarked that he was "hell on color" and said it when referring to the Music Pavilion, known affectionately to generations of New Yorkers as "the Old Bandstand." The watercolor faithfully reconstitutes the pagoda's elaborate color scheme, which was detailed in a description several paragraphs long appearing in an early guidebook. Authors' watercolor.

Opposite: The cast-iron Music Pavilion was, remarkably, originally designed to float in the Lake before Bethesda Terrace. Olmsted soon thought the wiser of his idea and the Moorish/Chinoiserie fantasy was sited beside the Mall and became a focal point of Manhattan civic life through the free concerts offered there throughout the summer months.

painting, or in the words of the English poet William Mason, with "a Poet's Feeling, and a Painter's eye." Consequently, theorists of the English landscape school made constant reference to the influential landscapes of Claude Lorrain, Nicolas Poussin and Salvator Rosa, and later to the importance of the Hudson River School in America.

The Greensward plan and its written explanation show that Olmsted and Vaux had mastered the principles of landscape composition underlying the English school. It must also be stated that they were the only competitors to do so; those few entries that rose above amateur status were characterized by ad hoc plans lacking any unity of vision, with features dotted about essentially random landscapes. Both Olmsted and Vaux were convinced that the unity and cohesiveness of a pastoral landscape was essential to the achievement of their shared vision for the park.

Olmsted in particular believed this with a near-missionary fervor and allowed formal elements with extreme reticence. In 1870, he gave a lecture in Boston on the subject of public parks, and the transcript of his remarks illuminates the talismanic power the pastoral landscape held upon him—a power that can only be adequately explained as a cipher for the beloved bucolic landscape of his Connecticut boyhood. As if to protect the sanctity of that vision, Olmsted waxed poetic with a reflexive but entirely unnecessary defense of the pastoral æsthetic—describing a frankly cloying Romantic tableau of "dainty cows and flocks of black-faced sheep"—when it came time to justify the inclusion of a formal promenade in a park's scheme:

> A Promenade may, with great advantage, be carried along the outer part of the surrounding groves of a park; and it will do no harm if here and there a broad opening among the trees discloses its open landscapes to those upon the promenade. But recollect that the object of the latter for the time being should be to see congregated human life under glorious and necessarily artificial conditions, and the natural landscape is not essential to them; though there is no more beautiful picture, and none can be more pleasing incidentally to the gregarious purpose, than that of beautiful meadows, over which clusters of level-armed sheltering trees cast broad shadows, and upon which are scattered dainty cows and flocks of black-faced sheep, while men, women, and children are seen sitting here and there, forming groups in the shade, or moving in and out among the woody points and bays.

To Olmsted's mind, a formal promenade was a dangerous thing indeed and must be handled quite gingerly if it were to "do no harm." Nonetheless, he and Vaux conceived the Mall to be the physical heart of Central Park, and they explained their reasoning in their written explication accompanying the Greensward plan:

> Although averse on general principles to a symmetrical arrangement of trees, we consider it an essential feature of a metropolitan park, that it should contain a grand promenade, level, spacious, and thoroughly shaded. The result can in no other way be so completely arrived at, as by an avenue, which in itself even, exclusive of its adaptability for this purpose, contains so many elements of

Opposite: A winter view of the Mall looking south, the formally planted allée of American elms creating a living cathedral. Sadly, due to the devastation of Dutch elm disease, Central Park's is among the largest such stands remaining in the country. Originally called the Promenade and also named Literary Walk because of the several sculptures of writers set along its southern end, the Mall presents a particular monochrome beauty during winter storms. Authors' watercolor.

Opposite: John Quincy Adams Ward's The Indian Hunter *remains among the finest sculptural ornaments of Central Park. Dedicated in 1869, the statue is one of four by this highly regarded sculptor to grace the park and is sited near Literary Walk at the Mall's southern end. Authors' watercolor.*

Above: The Mall's magnificent American elms in their early maturity. Originally planted with young, mature trees, the Mall suffered decimating losses, and saplings were used to fill the void. The experience quelled public demands for immediate landscape effects in the park.

grandeur and magnificence, that it should be recognized as an essential feature in the arrangement of any large park.... This avenue may be considered the central feature in our plan for laying out the lower park, and the other details of arrangement are more or less designed in connection with it.

At this point contradictions arise and the designers contend that however "essential" and "central" a formal promenade was to their scheme, it nevertheless should not constitute a "leading feature" of the design:

> The whole topographical character of the park is so varied, so picturesque, so individual in its characteristics that it would be contrary to common sense to make the avenue a leading feature, or to occupy any great extent of ground for this special purpose. It must be subservient to the general design, if that general design is to be in accordance with the present configuration of the ground, and we have therefore thought that it should, so far as possible, be complete in itself.

These conflicting statements reflect the fundamental unease with which Olmsted and Vaux viewed the use of formal elements such as the Mall, but nonetheless the partners recognized that "a grand mall, or open air hall of reception" was an essential—or perhaps unavoidable—element of their scheme, and they further stated that it "should occupy the same position of relative importance in the general arrangement of the plan that a mansion should occupy in a park prepared for private occupation."

With this explanation, the motive underpinning Olmsted and Vaux's creative process is made explicit: Central Park—at least its lower half—was conceived as an English manor park, with Scholars' Gate at Fifth Avenue and 59th Street its entrance, the gentle sweep of East Drive its approach, the formal grove of American elms at the Mall its phantom manse, Bethesda Terrace its garden terrace, the Lake its ornamental watercourse, the Ramble its wood and the Belvedere its distant folly-tower. Thus, it is deeply resonant when Olmsted and Vaux aver that the visitor "in the best sense is the true owner" of the park. Frederick B. Perkins, author of an early park guide, wrote perceptively of the Mall in 1864:

> This is the Heart of the Park; its richest and most elaborate scene. It was judged that, for this great democratic pleasure ground, such a scene, open to the sky, was far more appropriate than the close exclusiveness of a house. In this place would have been put the mansion of the gentleman or the castle of the baron, had such owned the Park. It is the Democratic Palace.

This grand scheme is oriented along a northwesterly axis two-thirds of a mile long, aligning the Mall and its pendant Terrace to the Belvedere and Vista Rock in the distance. Olmsted and Vaux crafted a classic course through a classically designed pastoral land-scape, in Vaux's words drawing visitors "out of the city into the park with the least delay possible" while guiding them through a varied and carefully planned series of tableaux to the center of the park grounds. They also mitigated the park's narrowness and exagger-ated its apparent extent by means of this ruling axis' diagonal orientation.

Page 46: Calvert Vaux's unique cast-iron and wood benches and a graceful canopy of American elms lend the Mall its unique poise. Photograph by Andrew Zega.

Preceding page: Initially, these monumental vases of polished rose granite, along with Mould's fanciful birdcages, marked the corners of the Concert Ground at the Mall's northern end. Authors' watercolor.

Above: One of the park's original water fountains, dispensing fresh Croton water, and at far left one of Mould's elaborate birdcages.

Opposite: Mould designed these "elaborate cages for birds of rich plumage" in 1864. Authors' watercolor.

The Musicians' Pavilion

Once known fondly to New Yorkers as "the Old Bandstand," the Musicians' Pavilion was one of Central Park's most familiar landmarks and the focal point of civic life on the Mall from the post–Civil War era until the promise of the Naumburg Bandshell precipitated its destruction in 1922. In a remarkable flight of fancy, Olmsted and Vaux originally envisioned the exotic pagoda moored in the Lake near Bethesda Terrace but dismissed the idea in favor of a prominent site at the northwest edge of the Mall promenade, not far from Bethesda Terrace. Jacob Wrey Mould's initial design for the floating, cast-iron pavilion, hardly altered in execution, was incontestably his most outlandish design for the park. The hexagonally planned pagoda featured eclectic but predominantly Moorish details and was clothed in Mould's characteristic chromatic flamboyance—a folly in the truest sense and an unexpected touch of Oriental opulence in nineteenth-century Manhattan.

The watercolor illustrated on page 39 follows Mould's original plans and its color scheme duplicates a detailed color description which Perkins required several paragraphs to explicate. He also paints a lively picture of the Old Bandstand's animating presence:

> Near the [Mall's] upper end we come to the Music-stand, a remarkably pretty structure, where, twice a week, a first-rate band performs, and makes an attraction which, on a fine day, draws immense crowds. The Music-stand itself is decorated with colors and gilding after a design by Mr. Jacob Wrey Mould, a gentleman to whom … the public is indebted for almost all the decorative work in the Park, and without whose help the Terrace, especially, could hardly have become the attraction it has proved. Just beyond the Music stand we reach the end of the Mall, which opens upon an ample rectangle of gravel, ornamented with two fountains, with gilded bird-cages, and with two extremely pretty drinking-basins. On music-days when the sun is oppressive, this square is covered with a light awning, and set with benches, where ladies and children gather and eat creams and ices to the "Minuet" in Don Juan, or "Le sabre de mon père."

At the outset, the Mall concerts generated controversy, with many predicting they would attract undesirable elements—specifically, the working classes and unionists—inciting a breakdown of public order. Those fears proved unfounded and newspaper accounts unanimously praised these enormously popular entertainments.

The Mall Birdcages and the Concert Ground

The remarkable birdcages illustrated here were designed by Mould in 1864 and once graced the Concert Ground at the Mall's northern end. Set at intervals between yew hedges, the cages have long since been destroyed, and the loss of the Old Bandstand and a pair of circular basins that graced the locale, as well as the placement of the Naumberg Bandshell, have muddled the area's logic and symmetry. Originally, the site was organized by rectangular plots lined with wooden benches, with Mould's birdcages and large, polished granite vases punctuating their corners. Together, these elements elaborated a cross-axis between the Old Bandstand to the west of the Mall and the Wisteria Pergola to its east. The Concert Ground, in turn, aligned with and offered a smooth transition to the Terrace precinct.

Opposite: Mould's early, unexecuted design for the birdcages embellishing the Mall. Authors' watercolor.

BETHESDA TERRACE

Of all I have ever done, it is perhaps the only thing that gives me much encouragement that I have in me the germ of an architect.

Calvert Vaux, writing of Bethesda Terrace

ON SEPTEMBER 16, 1858, the Park's board of commissioners approved the final scheme for Bethesda Terrace, the architectural centerpiece of Central Park and one of the grandest civic architectural achievements in nineteenth-century America. The elaborate complex was the built exception to Vaux's dictum that nature ranked first and second in the park's design, followed by architecture, but "only after a while." If it had been possible, Vaux wrote to the art critic Clarence Cook in 1865, he would have preferred a natural focus for the park, which he found void of any compelling topographical focal point. Instead, the elaborately ornamented architecture of Bethesda Terrace became the park's centerpiece and Vaux's most famous legacy, where his collaboration with the ornamentalist Jacob Wrey Mould—responsible for designing the structure's decorative details—reached its apogee.

Though terraces serving as transitional spaces between manor and garden had been common in European landscaping practice for centuries, most notably with Italian Renaissance villas and English country houses, Vaux's configuration of Bethesda Terrace—a fully independent structure set within the fabric of the park—was a complete novelty, explained by the designers' conception of the Mall, which was to play the role of the manor house ordering the entire Greensward scheme, with the Terrace as a dependency to this phantom building.

Stylistically, the Terrace's inspired admixture of ornament and historical reference was a high-water mark of Victorian eclecticism. While the Terrace's ancestry ultimately leads to the princely gardens of Italy and it was identified as an "Italian terrace" on the Greensward plan, the clearest formal precedent is the architect Jules Hardouin-Mansart's famed Orangerie at the Château de Versailles (p. 56), erected for Louis XIV between 1684 and 1686. Detached from the château itself, the Orangerie is an immense basement structure with overscaled arched windows, bracketed by the so-called Hundred Steps—two long flights of stairs which flank a central parterre and fountain and descend toward the large formal water basin known as the Pièce d'Eau des Suisses.

The Park's Architectural Centerpiece

In Olmsted and Vaux's first designs for Central Park, a terrace was only one of several competing concepts for the area immediately north of the Mall, and Conservatory Water was their first choice for the site of an Italianate arcade (p. 31). Commissioner Robert Dillon had even proposed to forego any important construction at the spot, and the terrace scheme only gradually gained prominence as planning progressed. Construction began soon after the park's board of commissioners approved the final design in September 1858 and greater funds became available as New York City prospered during the Civil War; though the board fully supported the high cost of the Terrace's extensive

Preceding page: A pair of piers bracket the flight of steps which link the northern terminus of the Mall and the Terrace's lower Arcade. That to the east is carved with ingenious allegorical sculptures representing Day, and that to the west, Night. The three unencumbered faces of both piers are carved with trefoil oculi sheltering allegorical scenes; here, one of three depictions of Night. Authors' watercolor.

Opposite: Sculpted by Emma Stebbins and dedicated in 1873, The Angel of the Waters *is the crowning sculpture of Bethesda Fountain. Depicting the angel who blessed the pool of Bethesda in the Gospel of John, the bronze figure symbolizes and celebrates the purity of the city's water supply upon completion of the Croton Aqueduct system. Authors' watercolor.*

ornamentation and intricate stonework (executed in the warm, grey Nova Scotia sand-stone of which Vaux was inordinately fond), the commissioners could not justify the cost of the numerous sculptures which Vaux hoped would enrich the scheme (seen in Mould's rendering, *opposite*) and left their funding to private subscriptions which never materialized. Though certain piers are topped with flat socles ready to receive figures (*p. 66*), those lining the upper viewing concourse received "temporary" capstones (*p. 73*).

The structure, largely completed in 1864, had been designated bridge no. 1, and when approved, the commissioners' minutes for 1858 described it as "the bridge, corridor and water-terrace at the north end of the Promenade." In the period before the dedication of Bethesda Fountain in May of 1873 determined its name for posterity, Bethesda Terrace was known both as the Water Terrace and the Terrace Bridge, this plethora of early appellations reflecting its hybrid form. Indeed, the Terrace is the most elaborate implementation of Olmsted and Vaux's principle of separating foot, equestrian and carriage traffic: A broad flight of stone steps at the northern termination of the Mall (*pp. 58, 66–67*) leads to the magnificent lower Arcade, its ceiling clad in Minton tiles (*pp. 74, 75*), which in turn leads to the lower plaza (*pp. 13, 59, 62–63*), making it unnecessary to cross Terrace Drive to reach the Lake and Bethesda Fountain.

Envisioned as the civic heart of Central Park on the cusp of the Civil War, the Terrace also became a symbol of the victorious Union and the liberal values it embodied. So it was that, despite its aristocratic forbearer, Vaux promoted the design as "essentially Republican in its inspiration and general conception," the heart of "the great art work of the Republic" and accessible to everyone in New York. As he wrote in the park's sixth annual report for 1862,

> The United States Flag will be introduced in a position with reference to the Park generally surmounting the rough stone outlook [Belvedere Castle] proposed to be built on the rock at the north end of the Ramble, on the direct vista line from the central walk of the Mall, and thus situated, it will also be the culminating point of interest in the view both from the upper and the lower terrace.

Opposite: A view of the Orangerie and Château de Versailles with the large reflecting basin known as the Pièce d'Eau des Suisses in the foreground. Oil painting by Pierre-Denis Martin, circa 1710. Musée Lambinet, Versailles.

Above: A panoramic lithograph of Bethesda Terrace executed after a drawing by Mould in 1864. Careful examination reveals the many bronze figures that Vaux had intended to crown numerous piers.

As the Terrace itself gained in importance, so its sculptural program also grew increasingly elaborate; Vaux intended that it "be as full of playful suggestion and liberal decoration in detail as the nature of the case will admit." The Terrace owes its decorative abundance to the singular figure of Jacob Wrey Mould, an extraordinarily talented and fecund ornamentalist with a flamboyant and controversial character. For inspiration, Mould turned to Gothic ecclesiastical architecture, which relied heavily on a unified pictorial program linking figural and ornamental sculpture, stained-glass windows and heraldic emblems—of which the Terrace's stylized sculptural ornaments are distant relatives—to convey moral teachings and metaphysical ideas. But it was Mould's particular artistic sensibility that shaped the structure's ornamental exuberance, which became much more than the sum of its decorative parts: The Terrace celebrates nature's bounty, diversity and harmony—a sculptural microcosmos of both the park itself and the country beyond, a Peaceable Kingdom where even the smallest element plays its role, reflecting the divine order and imbuing nature with intimations of Paradise.

Vaux and Mould introduced order and meaning to the ornamental program by employing the classical device of allegorical series, a common ordering principle in the decorative arts since the Renaissance. For example, the four seasons guided design of the Terrace's sculptural highlight—the intricate bas-relief panels of lyrically entwined foliage, interspersed with birds, insects and small mammals, which grace the baroquely figured retaining walls framing the stairs (*pp. 13, 72*). Of them Clarence Cook stated, "On no public building in America has there yet been placed any sculpture so rich in design as this, or so exquisitely delicate in execution."

Though near universally praised, Mould's work at the Terrace elicited a remarkably militant critique from the architect Peter B. Wight in 1863. Wight employed John Ruskin's principles of artistic authenticity to lambast the upper Terrace's ornament, remarking that it was "not only very conventional but much of it borders on the grotesque ... [the carvings are] merely clever copies of office drawings, by men who are degraded by being made the machines to carve other men's designs." Severe but fair, Wight offered high praise for the "easy, graceful and natural" sprays of foliage, fruit, flowers and berries that grace the centers of the balustrade panels lining the stairs, where he saw—correctly—that, following Ruskinian precepts, the

sculptors had been given free rein to execute the decorations without following a drawn template, thereby imbuing them with spontaneity and vitality of expression.

Wight certainly would have disapproved of the pair of piers that marked the northern end point of the Mall and which Vaux intended to serve as socles for bronze statues incarnating Day and Night (p. 66). Elaborate sculptural niches depicting emblematic scenes were carved into the three unencumbered faces of each pier. The eastern pier sports allegories of Day: the rising sun, a crowing rooster and a farmstead at harvest. To the west and the setting sun, the Night pier carries tableaux of an opened Bible and an oil lamp, an owl and a bat (p. 53) and the surprise of a witch on a broomstick flying above a jack-o'-lantern and below a crescent moon. Likewise, bronzes depicting the four ages of man were to top the four major piers at the heads of the staircases leading to the lower esplanade, and personifications of the four seasons were to grace the plinths on the landings below. Other series were to include The Mountain, The Valley, The River and The Lake, and the inevitable pairing of Art and Science. Vaux intended that the subterranean Arcade shelter the most elaborate group: four marble statues depicting Flora, Pomona, Sylva and Ceres were to be set in arched recesses, "in an architectural composition that will form a centre

Opposite: The flight of steps leading from the southern end of Bethesda Terrace's Arcade to the Mall during a winter snow. Photograph by Alfredo Bergna.

Above: The Bethesda Fountain, crowned by The Angel of the Waters, *seen through the northern end of the Terrace Arcade. Photograph by Noel Y. Calingasan.*

to the four and a background to each," crowned with a vase "filled with sculpted flowers, fruits, forest leaves, and grasses"; a glazed overhead light well was to bathe the elaborate ensemble in "a tempered light [which would] appear to emanate from it."

"J. Wrey Mould, universal genius"

Like Vaux, Mould, an Englishman, immigrated to New York in 1852, apparently at the behest of Moses H. Grinnell, a successful merchant and future park commissioner, to design the Unitarian Church of All Souls. Mould had apprenticed under Owen Jones, the great Victorian ornamentalist and author of *The Grammar of Ornament*, executing the plates of his monumental volume documenting the decoration of the Alhambra (which would later become his æsthetic touchstone). He also had assisted Jones in his position as superintendent of works for London's epochal Great Exhibition of 1851. An accomplished pianist and organist and a habile linguist, Mould published more than a dozen translations of Italian, German and French opera libretti while still in England.

At first, Mould was quite successful in New York; his flamboyance initially advanced his standing as a society architect, and he drew upon a vast knowledge of European

styles and ornaments—particularly the Spanish and Moorish designs he had drawn for Jones—when executing public and private commissions. Mould and Vaux soon fell in together in the city's small architectural community and, despite misgivings that the park competition would be politically decided, Mould assisted Vaux and Olmsted in preparing the Greensward presentation in the winter of 1857–1858. He drew innumerable trees and notably designed a magnificent octagonal formal garden with its Italianate Arcade (p. 31).

When the Greensward plan won the competition, Mould accepted the position of Vaux's assistant; in 1860, his patron Grinnell joined the park's board and Mould's prospects appeared sanguine. A collaborator as much as an assistant to Vaux and later for a time his partner in designing the initial master plan for the Metropolitan Museum of Art and the American Museum of Natural History, Mould was an idiosyncratic and talented designer responsible for several of the park's most remarkable built features, including the Sheepfold (p. 201), the Old Bandstand (p. 39) and the Menagerie (p. 145). However, when it became known in 1861 that he was living with a woman out of wedlock, he began an inexorable descent into the cruel moral universe of "the old New York code" mapped by Henry James and Edith Wharton, being "cut, quietly but firmly" by friends and acquaintances who were nonetheless fully cognizant of his exceptional talents.

In the spring of 1874, Henry Stebbins, president of the park's board, fired Mould, citing economy, though doubtless the real reasons were his adultery and having thrown his lot with the Tammany Hall regime, accepting the chief architect's post during the Sweeny board's short-lived ascendancy a few years prior. Several editorialists rose to Mould's defense and criticized the sacking as "a public scandal and an indecency" and

Above: Bethesda Terrace's western entry to the Mall viewed from Terrace Drive, 1869. Mould's Music Pavilion (p. 39) stands on axis in the distance, bracketed by the birdcages (p. 51) glimpsed behind the innermost piers (p.73).

Opposite: Venetian gondoliers posing before the nearly completed Bethesda Terrace during the Civil War. Note that the large socle (p. 208) seen behind the gondolier at left is still without its bronze mast.

Following pages: Bethesda Terrace during a winter snow. Photograph by Cornelis Verwaal.

Pages 64, 65, 68, 69: Bethesda Terrace is unified and delimited by balustrades comprised of square panels accented by richly ornamented piers. The panels are carved in a range of geometric patterns; this bold series borders Terrace Drive. Authors' watercolors.

Pages 67–67: Theme and variations. A composite view of the balustrades framing the stair providing access to the Terrace's sunken Arcade from the northern termination point of the Mall. Photograph by Andrew Zega.

"a shame and a disgrace." However, Clarence Cook wrote privately that "Mould owes a great deal of the ill treatment he complains of to himself" and that "On the social and moral side, it must have been hard for [the park's Puritanical comptroller] Mr. Green to have Mould about him at all." Though indefatigable and exceptionally talented, the architect was a spendthrift and an inveterate borrower, as well as "excessively egotistical"; but paramount and unforgivably, he lived in sin. In a profession dependent upon social interaction, colleagues and clients "could not ask him to their homes, and their families could never visit his." Prominent New Yorker, Mould creditor and diarist George Templeton Strong encapsulated and damned him for posterity as "that ugly and uncouth but very clever J. Wrey Mould, universal genius."

Mould eventually regained his post but, his position precarious, sought opportunity elsewhere. He found it in the person of Henry Meiggs, a flamboyant tycoon who had built the trans-Andean railroad and who had lately convinced the town fathers of Lima, Peru, to erect a vast public park. Mould spent four years in Lima, laying out the Parque de la Reserva and designing numerous private residences, and the period was the most fruitful episode of his colorful career, though his masterful decorative work for Central Park remains his foremost legacy. He died, virtually forgotten, in Manhattan in 1886. As Jervis McEntee, the Hudson River School painter and Vaux's brother-in-law, eulogized him,

he was a man of talent and had many genial traits, but without moral sense.... We were very intimate at one time, but his behaviour has been such that I could not recognize him and have had the pain of passing him in the street as

a stranger, which seems a cruel thing to do. He died almost friendless I learn, although the woman he called his wife stuck to him to the last.

The Angel of the Waters

Bethesda Fountain (*pp. 13, 59, 77*) is the focal point of the Terrace complex—Vaux referred to it as "the centre of the centre"—and despite the axial alignment of the distant tower of Belvedere Castle and its American flag (*p. 79*), it is the true culmination point of the great axis of the Mall. The three-tiered basin is loosely modeled upon the pair of fountains designed by Jacques Ignace Hittorff for the Place de la Concorde in Paris, the Fontaine des Fleuves and the Fontaine des Mers, both dedicated in 1840. Though it was the most important sculpture in the park, the fountain's crowning figure was not put to competition; rather Henry Stebbins, board president and chairman of the Standing Committee on Structures, Architecture and Fountains, saw to it that the commission fell to his sister Emma, an expatriate sculptress who lived and worked in Rome. The commissioners voted $8,000 to fund the figure's development, but the cost of casting the bronze was to be raised by private donations; fortunately, Stebbins was also head of the New York Stock Exchange and graciously underwrote this expense.

Vaux had specified that the bronze "should suggest both earnestly and playfully the idea of that central spirit of 'Love' that is for ever active, and for ever bringing nature, science, and art, summer and winter, youth and age, day and night, into harmonious accord," and Emma Stebbins' response was *The Angel of the Waters* (*p. 55*), a winged

Preceding page: Large rectangular piers such as this order the Terrace's extensive, figural borders. Authors' watercolor.

Opposite: Bethesda Terrace is actually the park's most elaborate bridge, allowing pedestrians walking from the Mall to reach the fountain and lower esplanade through this magnificently ornamented Arcade. Photograph by John Groenendijk.

Below: The Terrace Arcade is richly decorated with trompe l'œil pietra dura wall panels and a Minton-tiled ceiling. Photograph by Dana Hunting.

female figure whose striding pose and billowing drapery are modeled upon the Louvre's renowned antique fragment, the *Nike of Samothrace*. Ingeniously, small jets spray from the rocky base upon which the angel treads, creating the illusion that the bronze figure, originally gilded, appears to float above the fountain on a cloud of mist, evoking the account in the Gospel of John of an angel "troubling" the stagnant pool of Bethesda, miraculously imparting healing powers to the water. Fortunately, Stebbins had abandoned Vaux's hackneyed invocation of Love and developed a poetic and deeply resonant signification for the sculpture, alluding to the modern miracle of pure water supplied by the Croton water system. She had written,

> An angel descending to bless the water for healing seems not inappropriate in connection with a fountain, for although we do not have sad groups of blind, halt, and withered waiting to be healed by the miraculous advent of the angel, we have no less healing, comfort, and purification, freely sent to us through the blessed gift of pure, wholesome water, which to all the countless homes of this great city, comes like an angel visitant, not at stated occasions only, but day by day.

Less felicitous, however, was the figure's execution. Though angels are male by defi-nition, Stebbins' sculpture is female, its features modeled upon her companion, the famed American actress Charlotte Cushman. Further complicating gender matters, the figure often has been criticized as overtly masculine, as well as stiffly posed and clumsily executed. "There was a positive thrill of disappointment" when the sculpture was unveiled, the *Times* reported maliciously, and its critic remarked that "The head is distinctly a male head of a classical commonplace, meaningless beauty, the breasts are feminine, the rest of the body is in part male and in part female." Other contemporary critics were more generous; Cook, writing in the *Tribune,* was reminded of a depiction of the Archangel Gabriel by Raphael and "two or three early Italian pictures of the Annunciation." Sagely, neither Vaux nor Olmsted ever commented publicly on the work of their patron's sister. Despite enduring critical disfavor, *The Angel of the Waters* has remained a favorite park feature with the public since its unveiling and its abiding popularity has lent Bethesda Terrace its common name.

Above: Four large vases holding blooming plants in summer months are set atop the massive retaining walls bracketing the Terrace's twinned stair ramps. Authors' watercolor.

Opposite: Fountain in Central Park, *George Bellows' haunting 1905 oil sketch. Hirshhorn Museum and Sculpture Garden, Smithsonian Institution.*

IV   THE BELVEDERE

From here the Park may be seen spread like a panorama at your feet.

The Illustrated and Historical Souvenir of Central Park, 1893

THE BELVEDERE, A MINIATURE CASTLE built of grey Manhattan schist, is Central Park's grandest folly, sited atop Vista Rock—the park's second-highest elevation—to the north of the Ramble and pierced by the 79th Street Transverse Road. A belvedere or lookout tower was a required element of the park's competition program, and Olmsted and Vaux responded by proposing a crenellated stone tower at Vista Rock (*p. 28*) as well as a Ruskinian Gothic Observatory for the park's third-highest elevation, Great Hill near West 105th Street—though today mature shade trees and the surrounding Upper West Side have obscured that site's once-sweeping views of the Hudson River and its Palisades. The Observatory (*pictured above*) was never built, and construction of the Belvedere was delayed until after the close of the Civil War, when it was incorporated into an ambitious program of new amenities—including the Dairy, the Mineral Springs Pavilion, the Casino, the Children's Shelter, the Boys' and Girls' playhouses, and the projected Conservatory and Zoo—undertaken in the expansive period after Olmsted and Vaux were reappointed as the park's landscape architects in July of 1865.

Preceding page: The south elevation of Belvedere Castle. Authors' watercolor.

Above: Vaux's competition rendering of the stillborn Observatory, a Ruskinian Gothic tower proposed for the Great Hill.

Opposite: John Bachmann's View of Central Park, 1875. At center is Bethesda Terrace, to the left the Boathouse and at right Bow Bridge. The Belvedere, at left foreground, is drawn out of position, as its tower aligns with the axis of the Mall and Bethesda Terrace.

The importance of Vista Rock to the conception of the Greensward plan cannot be understated, for Olmsted and Vaux organized the lower half of Central Park about this immovable object. The massive outcrop had already been incorporated into the southwest corner of the Receiving Reservoir, which had ultimately determined the placement of the park itself, and in Mathew Brady's 1857 photograph, which Olmsted and Vaux incorporated into their submission (*p. 28, bottom*), a fire tower built by the Croton Aqueduct Board already stands on the promontory. Olmsted and Vaux retained the idea of a tower for the site and oriented the Mall and Bethesda Terrace to align with it, creating a diagonal, northward axis two-thirds of a mile long.

This grand ensemble, completed in the aftermath of the Civil War, culminates with the symbol of the nation united. A flagpole bearing aloft a large American flag was an integral element of the Belvedere's design, for the flag was the visual climax of this sweeping northward axis and was to be first glimpsed from the esplanade of Bethesda Terrace. A quite literal eye-catcher, the diminutive Belvedere and its outsized flag were intended to draw visitors from the formal precincts of the Mall and Terrace, across the Lake by way of Bow Bridge (conceived specifically for this purpose) and through the wilderness of the Ramble to the Belvedere's esplanade; mounting Belvedere Castle's tower, they are rewarded with expansive vistas of the entirety of the park. These exceedingly formalistic moves were axiomatic elements of both English and Continental landscape design; just as water was used as an animating force, carefully sited follies and eye-catchers were used as a motive force to draw visitors through varied landscape scenes.

Above: The Belvedere viewed from the Receiving Reservoir, which incorporated Vista Rock into its southwest corner.

Opposite, above: The initial scheme of the Belvedere, 1866. The Romanesque villa at center-left was canceled due to shifting budget priorities. Also note the crenellated tower and massively oversized flag and pole.

Opposite, below: Löwenburg Castle, a picturesque Medieval-revival pastiche of crumbling battlements sheltering palatial interiors, was erected by landgrave Wilhelm IX von Hessen in the late eighteenth century at the estate of Wilhelmshöhe in Hesse.

The Gothic revival was Vaux's preferred style and was launched by the singular figure of Horace Walpole, fourth earl of Orford and son of British Prime Minister Robert Walpole. Commencing in the late 1740s, Walpole recast his country seat of Strawberry Hill, an Elizabethan-era manor on the banks of the Thames, in a spirited, picturesque pastiche of the Tudor Gothic style. The enthusiasm for anything Medieval soon conquered the Continent, and a miniature fortress or evocative Medieval ruins became de rigueur garden ornaments for noblemen interested in pursuing the latest gardening trends. Beyond their undeniable picturesque qualities, neo-Gothic structures recalled chivalric values, offering an implicit critique of the reigning social order in Europe before the French Revolution.

The neo-Gothic style in turn spawned the Romanticism that would dominate the intellectual preoccupations of the early nineteenth century—a nearly universal movement that inspired literature and the arts and engendered the Hudson River School that was to shape the æsthetics of those responsible for the park's creation. At mid century, the writings of John Ruskin added tremendous impetus to the Gothic's continuing relevance. In Vaux's particular case, his 1847 Continental sketching tour with colleague George Truefitt was an important influence, particularly the Medieval architecture of the Rhine Valley, elements of which recur as a leitmotif throughout his later career, just as Olmsted's walking tour of England would fix itself upon his imagination. Though Vaux may not have visited Löwenburg Castle at Wilhelmshöhe in Kassel (*p. 82*), the picturesque folly, completed in 1801, is an early and exemplary model for the Belvedere.

Design, Construction and Politics
Vaux, assisted by Mould, designed the Belvedere from 1866 to 1867; the Croton Aqueduct Board ceded Vista Rock to the park in 1867, and the complex was completed four years later. The watercolor reproduced on pages 84—45 reconstitutes the north elevation of the original scheme, with Belvedere Castle at left and at right a pendant building—a Romanesque villa featuring an open, arcaded loggia, a corner tower capped by a conical slate roof and a stair descending to the parapet of the Receiving Reservoir, today Turtle Pond. This picturesque villa, designed in a fully distinct architectural style, was intended to balance and complement the Belvedere across a generous plaza and was to serve as a second belvedere, offering views of the park's northern reaches.

This structure was canceled in 1870 due to the shifting priorities of the incoming Tammany Hall regime, which chose to employ a massive (voting) labor force to prune, sod, straighten and plant floral arabesques in preference to funding brick-and-mortar projects. In 1871, during Vaux's second political exile, Mould—who had assumed his duties—convinced the short-lived Sweeny board to fund his grandiose Sheepfold (*p. 201*) to the detriment of Vaux's Belvedere villa, erecting a decorative wooden shed to fill the resultant void. Olmsted and Vaux had this "gaudily painted contrivance" demounted upon their return, intending to re-erect it in Mount Morris Park, only for it to be resurrected by the Conservancy in the late twentieth century.

The striking photograph illustrating page 82 reveals a forgotten aspect of the Belvedere's original setting—the old Receiving Reservoir and the vast expanse of water found to its north and east—and underscores the site's inherent visual power: to the north, the Belvedere suggested a picturesque Scottish castle perched above a loch; to the south, it evoked a fortified bastion built on a rocky promontory.

Opposite: The Belvedere today, viewed across Turtle Pond at the southern edge of the Great Lawn, both of which were completed in 1935 after the removal of the Receiving Reservoir. (It is revealing to compare this view to the early photograph reproduced on page 82.) From the outset, Belvedere Castle had served as an important meteorological station, and in 1919 the U.S. Weather Bureau closed the structure to the public and removed the tower's roof to accommodate its instruments. In the 1960s, automated equipment was installed nearby and the mutilated Belvedere was abandoned to vandals. Public outcry led to its restoration, completed by the City and the Conservancy in 1982. Photograph by Andrew Zega.

Following pages: Jacob Wrey Mould's bas-relief cockatrice decorates the overdoor of the entrance to Belvedere Castle. The cockatrice is a mythical chimera, a dragon with a rooster's head, which medieval Britons believed could kill with a glance. Authors' watercolor.

V CONSERVATORY GARDEN

It seemed almost like being shut out of the world in some fairy place.

Frances Hodgson Burnett, *The Secret Garden*

IN THEIR ORIGINAL GREENSWARD PLAN, Olmsted and Vaux envisioned an arboretum—a garden of native and exotic plants collected for botanical study and display, scientific and medicinal research and economic evaluation—occupying the eastern third of the park above the upper reservoir. A botanical garden of this scale would have been the largest in the United States, and the planners' impetus sprang from a reflexive Victorian belief in the arboretum's myriad civic virtues, and in truth any municipality of any pretension sought to establish its own botanical garden for public instruction and diversion, due in great part to the tireless proselytizing of Scotsman John Claudius Loudon, publisher and author of numerous horticultural tomes and journals and the era's most vocal and influential proponent of the value of botanical gardens.

Constrained by a restrictive budget, Olmsted and Vaux were forced to abandon the arboretum and recast the entirety of the park's northern reaches as rolling meadows interspersed with dense copses, giving over to a rustic, wooded wilderness highlighted by water features in the Harlem annex. Upon resuming their duties in 1865, they proposed a conservatory (p. 96) for the site of what is now Conservatory Water at Fifth Avenue at 74th Street. This structure was never executed, and the conservatory to which Conservatory Garden owes its name was finally erected in 1899, at the height of the City Beautiful movement Loudon had in part inspired, on the site of a working nursery that raised planting stock for the park grounds, located at upper Fifth Avenue at 105th Street. The three-tiered, cast-iron greenhouse became a favored promenade for society—the remote site having the coincidental advantage that it kept certain social elements at bay. However, by 1934 fashion and mores had irrevocably changed and the conservatory itself had fallen into disrepair, prompting park commissioner Robert Moses to order its demolition and the creation of an entirely new garden which opened to the public in 1937.

Moses confided Conservatory Garden's design to Gilmore David Clarke, an eminent civil engineer and landscape architect, seconded by M. Betty Sprout, charged with the planting schemes. Clarke conceived the clear, Beaux-Arts delineation of the garden's three major precincts, and Sprout crafted those spaces into richly detailed and highly distinctive gardens. A prominent gardener with a serendipitously Dickensian name, Sprout was an avid disciple of Gertrude Jekyll, the English horticultural revolutionary and creator of the herbaceous border. Jekyll saw gardening in painterly terms: the garden was an artistic composition, a richly interwoven arrangement of complementary and contrasting colors and textures, of flowers and foliage unfolding over the succession of the seasons. Sprout's planting schemes are masterful interpretations of Jekyll's precepts and are still today the glory and enchantment of Conservatory Garden.

Preceding pages: A detail of the Vanderbilt Gate, a wrought-iron masterwork that serves as entrance to the sheltered precincts of Central Park's magnificent formal garden, Conservatory Garden. Authors' watercolor.

Opposite: The Secret Garden, a bronze sculpture group executed by Bessie Potter Vonnoh and inspired by the characters Mary, Dickon and robin redbreast from Frances Hodgson Burnett's classic children's tale. The sculpture stands in a lily pond in the English Garden. Authors' watercolor.

Vanderbilt Gate (*detail, pp. 90–91*), a magnificent neo-baroque wrought-iron carriage gate located at Fifth Avenue and 105th Street, offers a fittingly majestic overture to this most formal of all the park's attractions. The gate originally guarded entry to Cornelius Vanderbilt II's mansion at Fifth Avenue and 58th Street, in its time the city's largest and grandest private residence. Designed by architects George B. Post and Richard Morris Hunt in 1882, the massive, red-brick château was demolished in 1927, supplanted by the Bergdorf Goodman department store. The imposing wrought-iron carriage gate, designed by Post and executed in France in 1894, was then donated to the city by Gertrude Vanderbilt Whitney and remounted in 1939.

The Italian Garden

A graceful flight of bowing limestone steps cascade to the level of a large, green rectangle of perfectly maintained lawn, neatly bordered by clipped yew hedge—inexplicably named the Italian Garden and the physical center of Conservatory Garden's six-acre enclosure. Doubled rows of crab apple, magnificent in bloom, flank the lawn and also delimit the three gardens comprising Conservatory Garden itself. To the south is the English or Secret Garden and to the north the French Garden. Flagstone paths edged with benches run beneath the crab apple allées and on spring days offer one of the park's most

Opposite: The theatrical perspective of Conservatory Garden's central Italian Garden in spring, punctuated by a single fountain jet and bordered by white-flowering crab apple allées. Authors' watercolor.

Above: A bird's-eye view of the Conservatory Garden in spring. Fifth Avenue runs at bottom, with the English Garden at left, the Italian Garden at center and the French Garden at right. Photograph by Sara Cedar Miller/ Central Park Conservancy.

enchanting spaces, the mature trees arched in bloom overhead, dappling the sunlight and shedding a slow, gentle rain of pink and white petals.

The Italian Garden's large lawn—more evocative of English bowling greens or French parterres, but no matter—guides the eye to the west where a simple water jet closes the main axis, the centerpiece of a terraced exedra crowned by a wisteria pergola. The long rectangle of lawn and the half-circle of the exedra create a basilican plan, among the most venerable and æsthetically pleasing of all classical forms. The exedra, like its Italian models, is sculpted from the flank of a low, forested ridge that defines the garden's western boundary and provides a verdant backdrop for this skillfully composed garden theater.

The French Garden

The French Garden to the north is incongruously abloom with Dutch tulips in spring and masses of Japanese chrysanthemums in autumn, with nary an *œillet* or marguerite in sight between-times, and the mystery of its name only deepens when one considers that formal French gardens are neither comprised of bedded flowers nor are they drawn upon elliptical plans. In fact, Le Nôtre despised flower gardens and would only design them at the royal behest. Nonetheless, the garden can be said to be French in that it is strictly geometrical and enclosed by a Japanese holly hedge, suggesting baroque bosquets and

95

hinting at the inward-looking *jardin clos* of the Renaissance, which mixed flowers and herbs in rectilinear beds cultivated behind high walls.

The Untermyer Fountain dominates the French Garden and stands at the center of a figural, oval-shaped formal pool, flanked by a pair of smaller jets. The actual fountain is a beswagged limestone drum which carries on its lip the bronze sculpture group *Three Dancing Maidens,* executed by the German sculptor Walter Schott, whose work was much prized by the imperial court in Berlin. Schott fused the ancient Greek myth and enduring artistic theme of the Charites, the three graces, goddesses of beauty (Aglaea), mirth (Euphrosyne), and good cheer (Thalia), with the equally venerable pagan myths of water nymphs and sylphs. The life-size bronze figures dance round the water jet with youthful exuberance, a lyrical tour de force of arrested movement whose great visual power dramatically counters the garden's otherwise staid composition.

The English Garden
The beloved English Garden, also known as the Secret Garden, is the one part of Conservatory Garden that indeed merits both its names. Sheltered by mature deciduous trees and ringed by lilacs and magnolias, the English Garden is drawn on a *demilune* plan and enchants with its intimate scale, its lush herbaceous borders and the idyllic lily pond at its center, the colorful koi swimming within shaded by a mature flowering crab apple.

The Secret Garden fountain, sculpted by Bessie Potter Vonnoh, stands at the far end of the elliptical basin and depicts the characters Mary and Dickon from Frances Hodgson Burnett's classic children's novel. Vonnoh was justly famed for her psychologically insightful sculptures and executed the bronze group in 1937, adding the reclining figure of Dickon to an earlier bronze entitled *Garden Figure* created in 1931.

Mary gazes across her shoulder at her feathered friend, robin redbreast, gracefully holding aloft a shallow bowl that serves as his birdbath. Real birds often join their bronze counterpart without ever perturbing Mary, transfixed by the music of Dickon's flute. Such is the decorous magic of the Secret Garden that, coming upon the scene in a rare moment of calm, one might feel an intruder who has stumbled upon a fairy tale come fleetingly to life and, if only for an instant, catch oneself so as not to disturb the children's reverie.

Above: The original design for the conservatory proposed for Conservatory Water was published in the park's 1871 Annual Report but was never built. In 1898, a greenhouse was finally constructed on the site of Conservatory Garden and lent the present garden its name.

Opposite: The Untermyer Fountain, centerpiece of the French Garden, crowned by Three Dancing Maidens, a bronze sculpture group executed by the German sculptor Walter Schott. Photograph by Jake Rajs.

VI LAKES, PONDS AND MEERS

*Here boys may fancy themselves at sea, and hope, by some
lucky accident, to taste the terrors of shipwreck.*

Clarence C. Cook, describing the Lake in 1869

WATER IS THE LIFEBLOOD OF A GARDEN. Indeed, taken to first principles, as Leon-ardo remarked, "water is the driving force of all nature" and a garden without water is but half a garden, for it lacks water's mutable, animating force. The first garden was cultivated at the site of a source, for Genesis tells us that "a river went out of Eden to water the garden." Water also determined the site of Central Park, or more accurately it was Nicholas Dean, president of the Croton Aqueduct Board, water's municipal representative, who ensured that a new reservoir vital to the city's continued expansion be located on city-owned land immediately to the north of the existing Receiving Reservoir—a vast, rectangular water fortress of rusticated stone stretching from 79th to 86th streets and from Sixth to Seventh avenues.

In 1851, while the nature, size and location of a large public park were being debated, Dean was the first to propose boundaries for a "central park" (some 600 acres bordered by Fifth and Seventh Avenues and 59th and 106th streets) largely following those ultimately adopted. The recently completed Croton Aqueduct system was a monumental feat of

Preceding pages: In the spring of 1860, the city of Hamburg gifted a dozen mute swans to the city of New York to ornament Central Park. Nine swans died soon after their arrival by steamer, and another ten were dispatched along with plans for floating nesting platforms, one of which is depicted here in its end elevation. Not to be outdone, the vintners and dyers guilds of London sent fifty swans upon learning of New York's loss. Authors' watercolor.

Above: The 1.6-mile-long footpath ringing the Jacqueline Kennedy Onassis Reservoir offers breathtaking panoramic views of the Manhattan skyline, here looking south toward Midtown. Authors' watercolor.

civil engineering and a great source of civic pride, and Dean's voice carried considerable weight in the debate over what was naturally seen as a successor public works project of rival ambition and extent. Though Dean's proposal could be construed as self-interested in that he foresaw the dual benefits of embellishing the existing Receiving Reservoir by ensconcing it within a pastoral landscape and substantially reducing the construction cost of the planned reservoir by uniting the project with that of the proposed park, the scheme had numerous advantages that attracted divergent interests (chief among them were the site's central location on the island, the low cost of the land and the relative paucity of vested economic interests attached to it, as well as the prohibitive cost of grading such unpromising land both for streets and building sites) and so ultimately triumphed.

It was the much-maligned Capt. Egbert Viele, the Army engineer who drew the park's first, insipid plan, who nonetheless had the good sense to sculpt the new reservoir's borders in a sinuous outline which all later competitors adopted. The massive, 106-acre sheet of water unavoidably acts to detach the northern third of the park into virtually a separate entity—it certainly has its own distinct character—and the Reservoir's raised banks were landscaped with a 1.6-mile-long promenade which today offers remarkable panoramic views of the city. There was nothing to be done with the existing Receiving Reservoir but plant heavily about it, its luster as a technological marvel having been eclipsed by its new neighbor. Its removal and the creation of the Great Lawn and Turtle Pond were carried out as a public works project during the Great Depression and this visionary scheme, overseen by Robert Moses and completed in 1937, reaffirmed the

101

guiding principles of the Greensward plan against an onslaught of competing proposals — among them a war memorial, an opera house, a stadium and a parking garage—and was the greatest positive transformation in the park's history.

Rendered obsolete upon completion of the city's Water Tunnel N° 3, the Reservoir was decommissioned in 1993 and renamed the year following to honor Jacqueline Kennedy Onassis, a tireless champion of historical preservation who enjoyed jogging there. Though various proposals for the Reservoir's reuse have been forwarded, the city and Conservancy have opted to maintain the status quo and most recently have replanted the straight drive known as Rhododendron Mile on the Reservoir's eastern flank.

Beside the obligatory reservoirs, Olmsted and Vaux proposed only two significant bodies of water in the Greensward plan: the Pond in the park's southeast corner and the Lake occupying its lower third, both of which resculpted existing streams. They also included a first version of the Pool, a small pond in the park's northern reaches, to be created by damming Montayne's Rivulet, a stream that skirted the base of Great Hill and tumbled northeasterly through the Ravine to Harlem Creek. With the Harlem annexation of 1863, the designers shifted the Pool southwest to its present location near Central Park West at

Above and opposite: The original Boathouse captured in photographs dating from the early twentieth century. Both images feature the silent electric boats that Olmsted had specified for the Lake, seen boarding passengers at the dock. These boats were discontinued in the 1920s and Vaux's Boathouse was demolished in 1952, to be replaced by the Loeb Boathouse.

101st Street and fashioned the Harlem Meer from the marshy lowlands at the head of the Harlem Creek at the park's northeastern tip.

The Lake

The pivotal element of the magisterial, carefully orchestrated entry sequence of placid Pond, Mall promenade, splendid Terrace, picturesque Lake, wild Ramble and distant Belvedere that Olmsted and Vaux crafted for the lower park, the 22-acre Lake is the park's largest open body of water and its scenic heart. Wonderfully varied vistas are to be had from any point on its shores or from the rowboats that ply its placid waters. The Lake is nearly divided in two at the site of Bow Bridge; the larger, western arm is oriented north to south and is edged with a rich assortment of scenic vantage points: the wooded mouth of the Gill, Bank Rock (*p. 107*) and Balcony bridges, the rocky Hernshead promontory (*p. 15*) and idyllic Wagner Cove (*p. 106*). The eastern arm is dominated by the esplanade of Bethesda Terrace (*p. 13*) and the Loeb Boathouse, which replaced Vaux's original Boathouse in 1954.

In 1870, Olmsted insinuated that the early completion of the Lake had saved the park itself from being abandoned. "At one time nearly four thousand laborers were employed;

Following pages: The Beresford Apartments seen through morning mist rising from the Lake in early spring.
The Ladies' Pavilion at Hernshead (p. 195) can be glimpsed at left and Bow Bridge at far right.
Photograph by Cornelis Verwaal.

103

and for a year at one point, work went on night and day in order to put it as quickly as possible beyond the reach of those who were bent on stopping it." Olmsted was dramatizing for effect, but his point is well taken; in 1858 an army of laborers toiled to transform the marshy south branch of the Saw Kill into the Lake in time for winter ice skating. Though the work was not completed until the following year, the basin was partially filled that December, inaugurating a rage for ice skating that at its peak brought 100,000 visitors a day and cemented the public's bond with the nascent park.

The Boathouse

Boating became popular in the summer months, and rowboats and gondolas with authentic Venetian gondoliers were available for hire, as well as two classes of silent, electrically driven passenger skiffs (an idea promoted by Olmsted) which called at six rustic boat landings spotted about the Lake's shores. Initially the boating concessions were run from a wooden dock beside the Terrace, but their popularity soon outstripped this makeshift arrangement, leading Vaux to design the original Boathouse (*pp. 102, 103*) in 1873. Constructed at the Lake's eastern tip and deliberately planned "on a liberal scale" to ensure that the Terrace would not later be enlisted as a boat landing, Vaux based the structure on the Refectory, a chalet-style wooden arcade he had designed in 1871 for the city of Buffalo's parade. The detailing, drawn by Mould and Julius Munchwitz, was a spirited pastiche of turned wood colonnettes and heavily ornamented board-and-batten panels. In Vaux's own words, the Boathouse's upper deck offered "an elevated promenade, from which a view of the water can be obtained, with a special charm of its own."

Above: The rustic boat landing at Wagner Cove is an idyllic spot nestled under mature shade trees. It can also be glimpsed in a period photograph at the top of page 34. Authors' watercolor.

Right: October in Central Park brings the russet colors of autumn. Oak Bridge spans Bank Rock Bay, the northernmost finger of the Lake, providing access to the Ramble from the park's west side. The largest and most elaborate of the park's wooden spans, Oak Bridge was rebuilt after Vaux's original design in 2009 with a steel substructure and a wooden deck and balustrades. Photograph by Cornelis Verwaal.

Left: Gapstow Bridge in winter looking toward the park's main entrance at Grand Army Plaza. Graceful Gapstow Bridge carries a footpath over the northern arm of the Pond and is one of the most photogenic structures in Central Park. Built of Manhattan schist, it replaced an earlier wooden bridge of the same name (p. 124) in 1896. Comparing this view with the photograph from the early 1930s appearing on page 37 reveals dramatic changes to the cityscape surrounding Grand Army Plaza in the intervening decades. Photograph by Fran Simó.

Conservatory Water

Recalling the famed octagonal basin in the Luxembourg Garden, where Parisian children have sailed model boats for centuries, Conservatory Water is a large, formal reflecting pond with a figured oval plan and low, cut-stone coping. Olmsted and Vaux had originally planned a formal garden and a viewing arcade (*p. 31*) for the site (near Fifth Avenue at 74th Street), but Commissioner Dillon favored a decorative pond at the location, a solution which had been proposed by several other competitors. The designers bowed to his wishes, intending that the basin serve as the reflecting pool for the conservatory housing tropical plants specified in the 1857 competition guidelines. Though it lent its name to the basin, that greenhouse was eventually erected on the site of Conservatory Garden in 1899. The charming Kerbs Memorial Boathouse, with its distinctive, high-pitched copper roof, was built in 1954, replacing an older wooden structure. It houses the model boats children of all ages sail on Conservatory Water as well as a simple café.

Harlem Meer

Harlem Meer recalls the city's Dutch heritage (*meer* is a Dutch word meaning lake) and anchors the park's northeast corner, and its eastern arm descends to touch Conservatory Garden's manicured grounds at the northern edge of the French Garden. The village of Harlem once lay just to the northwest, a Dutch enclave fittingly founded near the brackish wetlands which were dredged to form the Meer—at 14 feet above sea level the lowest point on Manhattan Island, a topography recalling the village's namesake city, Haarlem. Harlem was incorporated into New York City in 1873, a decade after the tract

Above: The Lake in winter with Central Park West's famed apartment buildings rising behind. At left, the Dakota and at center-right, the twin-spired Majestic. Photograph by Alfredo Bergna.

Opposite, above: The Lake for Miniature Yachts by American impressionist William Merritt Chase, 1888.

Opposite, below: Conservatory Water at the turn of the twentieth century with a skyline dominated by the dome of Temple Beth-El, demolished in 1947. The original wooden boathouse is seen at center.

from 106th to 110th streets had been annexed to the park. Comptroller Andrew Haswell Green, whose iron will and parsimony drove Olmsted and Vaux to resign their positions during the Civil War, oversaw construction of the ruggedly picturesque woodlands of the Harlem annex and closely followed the letter and spirit of their design. Originally fed by Montayne's Rivulet, which also had been dammed to form the Pool and feed the Loch, the Meer is now supplied by water piped from the Reservoir.

In 1966 Lasker Rink and Pool was constructed on the Meer's western arm, reducing its surface area to eleven acres and initiating an era of rapid decline. Extensive renovations were undertaken from 1988 to 1993; the Meer was re-dredged, concrete embankments were removed and its banks were extensively landscaped, and the Charles A. Dana Discovery Center was constructed on the site of the old boathouse, which vandals had reduced to ruins.

Designed to harmonize with Calvert Vaux's original park buildings, the Dana Center is the symbol of the northern park's renaissance and provides a visitor center and community programs. Far more sensitively sited and detailed than its predecessor, the satisfying mass of the building, framed by a weeping willow and reflected in the Meer's waters, offers an unexpected, indeed almost idyllic vision that leaves little regret for the loss of the Moses-era boathouse it replaces, harmonizing almost perfectly with the ideas that Olmsted and Vaux had harbored for this corner of the park.

Above: The Charles A. Dana Discovery Center enlivens the northern shore of Harlem Meer. Erected in 1993 and designed in the spirit of Calvert Vaux, the handsome building serves as a visitor and community center for the upper reaches of the park. Authors' watercolor.

Opposite: The Cascade (originally named "The Dripping Rocks") in the carefully composed wilds of the Ravine, a wooded escarpment traversed by the Loch, a stream linking the Pool to Harlem Meer. Photograph by Philip Haber.

VII   BRIDGES AND ARCHES

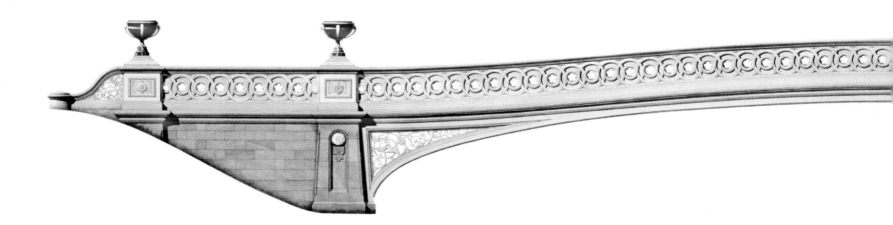

*For the most part our bridges are as ugly as our engineers, with
their dryasdust brains, can devise. But in the Park the effort was
made to have the bridges not only solidly built, but as elegantly,
and in as great a variety of designs, as could be contrived.*

Clarence C. Cook, "Central Park," 1873

E VERY GREAT GARDEN has a signature feature, a leitmotif that renders it unique and
reveals its creator's mastery and erudition. At first glance, this is often an invisible
quality, sometimes intangible but always omnipresent, that underlies and orders the
designer's creative process; Olmsted referred to it as "the motive"—the transcendent
ordering principle that acts like a compass to guide the designer in the alchemical process
of transforming raw terrain into the sublime experience of a successfully idealized landscape. The great gardens of France distinguish themselves through the order and poise
of geometry exercised on a godlike scale; England's landscape parks are justly celebrated
for pastoral compositions of unsurpassed subtlety and extent; and the gardens of Renaissance Italy remain eternal studies in the seductive fascination of philosophy expressed
in decorative scenography. Each of these traditions reflects the political, intellectual and
artistic preoccupations of its time, and it is no surprise that Central Park, "an American
masterpiece" as park photographer Sara Cedar Miller so fittingly described it, mirrors and
distills the ideas of a modern society during the expansive age of the Industrial Revolution.

The genius of Central Park resides here, in the application of the principles of innovation, efficiency and economy of scale that drove the rapid industrialization transforming
the northern states. To employ Olmsted's phrase, the motive underlying the park's inception was a rare consensus shared by all major actors that success was not to be measured
by any conventional yardstick but rather lay in anticipating the functional requirements of
a large public park and both integrating it with and sheltering it from the future heart of
one of the fastest growing cities of the nineteenth century.

The city's quickening expansion was evident to all and an overriding concern. It was
the simplest of calculations to project census figures documenting the city's explosive
population growth fifty years into the future; Downing's exhortation was typical when
he wrote in 1851 that New York was "the fourth city in the world (with a growth that will
soon make it the second), the commercial metropolis of a continent spacious enough to
border both oceans." In their written submission accompanying the Greensward plan,
Olmsted and Vaux stressed the same concerns, noting, "No longer an open suburb,
our ground will have around it a continuous high wall of brick, stone, and marble. The
adjoining shores will be lined with commercial docks and warehouses; steam boat and
ferry landings, railroad stations, hotels, theatres, factories, will be on all sides of it and
above it; all which our park must be made to fit."

The designers also cautioned against misplaced parsimony and restricted vision: "Up
to this time, in planning public works for the city of New York, in no instance has adequate
allowance been made for its increasing population and business; not even in the case
of the Croton Aqueduct, otherwise so well considered." Such penury and shortsighted

*Preceding pages: A watercolor
elevation of Bow Bridge, arguably the
defining architectural ornament of
Central Park. The graceful cast-iron
structure was designed by Vaux and
detailed by Mould and completed in
1862. It spans 60 feet between red
sandstone abutments and carries
pedestrians across the Lake, linking
Bethesda Terrace to the Ramble.
Authors' watercolor.*

*Opposite: The elegant, interlocking
guilloche pattern of Bow Bridge's
balustrades was a common
decorative motif in ancient Greco-
Roman architecture. With Victorian
insouciance, Jacob Wrey Mould
enriched the pattern's central
voids with Gothic cinquefoils.
Photograph by Anne Canright.*

half-measures could no longer be tolerated, for they would doom such a defining project to failure; Mayor Ambrose C. Kingsland was determined that the park "prove a lasting monument to the wisdom, sagacity and forethought of its founders, and would secure the gratitude of thousands yet unborn." With only slight exaggeration, Olmsted later stated that "In laying out Central Park we determined to think of no results to be realized in less than forty years."

The Greensward plan's true genius resides not primarily in æsthetics but in function—not in the *greensward* but in the *plan*. The original competition requirements were few and straightforward and offered no guidance in addressing these overriding yet implicit concerns: The park must provide "four or more crossings from east to west," a large parade ground, three playgrounds, a site reserved for a concert and exhibition hall, an imposing fountain, a prospect tower, a two- to three-acre flower garden and a skating pond. From that meager charge, Olmsted and Vaux crafted a plan that ensured Central Park's continuing relevance and ultimately its integrity by providing superior if not visionary functionality. It is quite probable that, lacking their ingeniously organized circulation plan, Manhattan's spectacular growth would have ensured that Central Park came down to us mutilated and unrecognizable. Their solution, their "motive," inspired by the recently completed Bois de Boulogne in Paris, was to ensure that pedestrian, equestrian and carriage traffic within the park remained separated and would never cross at grade. Most importantly, the transverse roads carrying crosstown traffic were to be set seven feet below grade, permitting all park traffic to be carried independently over them, thereby isolating "a turbid stream of coarse traffic, constantly moving at right angles to the

Above: Bow Bridge in winter, viewed across the Lake from Hernshead. Photograph by Raymond Larose.

Opposite: The intricate Victorian tracery of Pine Bank Arch, a cast-iron pedestrian bridge spanning the bridle path near West Drive at the level of 62nd Street. Photograph by John Blough.

Following pages: A watercolor elevation of Gothic Bridge, the famed cast-iron pedestrian bridge spanning the western leg of the bridle path near the Reservoir at the level of 94th Street. Authors' watercolor.

line of the park movement." If the principal objective of their work had been to display an impression of effortless harmony between the mundane demands of traffic flow and the Elysian requirements of an Arcadian landscape, Olmsted and Vaux could not have succeeded more spectacularly.

To camouflage these sunken thoroughfares, which otherwise would have destroyed the park's physical and æsthetic integrity by dividing it into five rectangular compartments, the transverse roads were lined with dense planting and bridged at irregular intervals by massive arches averaging 120 feet wide—spans sufficiently ample to carry the main park drives, the bridle path and footpaths while also providing room for a generous layout and planting screens, ensuring that these massive bridges melded imperceptibly with the surrounding landscape. Indeed, most visitors would be hard-pressed to identify the exact locations of the park's transverse roads.

This innovation had no direct precedent in garden design in either Europe or America, though cutting and grading was an engineering necessity when laying railroad rights of way, such as that of the New York & Harlem Railroad, among the nation's earliest, which by 1852 reached to Albany. Such a parallel would have been self-evident to Vaux, for whom engineering was essential to his work, and he is likely the design's author. However, the architect was so self-effacing that upon winning the competition he himself had brought into being, he accepted that Olmsted be named "architect-in-chief" while he was designated his "assistant"—even though Olmsted had no formal education beyond haphazard tutoring and a three-month dalliance at Yale. Transparently, Vaux later wrote:

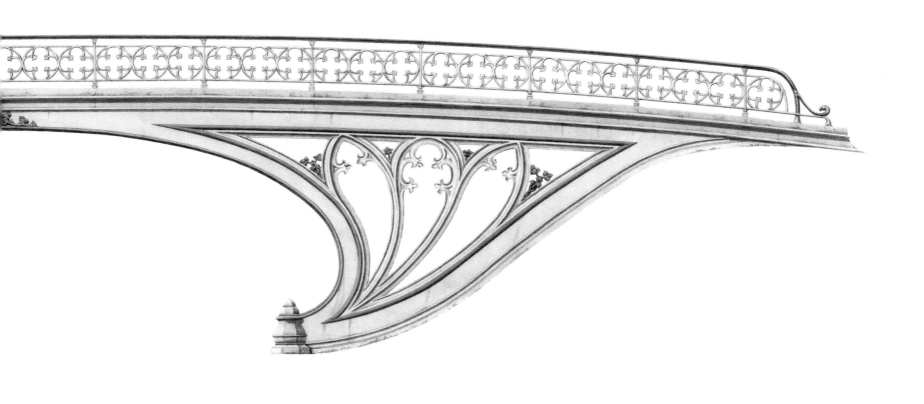

The idea of keeping the transverse roads for city traffic clear of the Park roads designed for pleasure driving was gradually developed by a close study of the actual typography and of the imperative future needs of the City, and its importance as an elemental feature being recognized before the plan was completed, it was tacitly agreed between the two partners that no individual claim should be made by either designer in regard to that particular feature.

Likewise, Vaux's experience assisting Downing in designing the Mall and Capitol grounds in Washington, D.C.—the former also a narrow, rectangular plot with numerous cross streets—offered the precedent of dense screening, and it would seem that the solution ultimately sprang from the immovable object of Vista Rock, the massive outcrop that had been integrated into the southwest corner of the Receiving Reservoir and which impeded the natural course of the 79th Street Transverse Road along the Reservoir's southern flank. Olmsted and Vaux proposed to tunnel through the outcrop, and it may well have been this idea, along with the vision of the transverse road set beside the Reservoir's raised stone berm, that together sparked the brilliant solution of sinking all the transverse roads in cuts and dissimulating them with heavily planted berms.

A Separation of Ways
Though both designers promoted the idea of the park as a natural oasis offering a respite from the "overwrought" city, they nevertheless saw no conflict in running footpaths "close

Above: Spur Rock Arch, a cast-iron bridge that once spanned the bridle path at the level of Seventh Avenue at 61st Street, was demolished in 1934 to permit expansion of Heckscher Playground. Sister of and model for Gothic Bridge, it was designed by Vaux with the assistance of Edward C. Miller and completed in 1861. Detail of a lithograph prepared for the commissioners' Third Annual Report of 1859.

Above and right: Befitting its function as a portal to the Mall precinct, Marble Arch was the most elaborate of all bridges erected in the park, providing a pedestrian arcade with inset benches, a demilune niche with a water fountain and mirroring flights of stairs along its north face. It was the only overtly classical structure designed by Vaux for the park and was foolishly destroyed in 1938 when Center and East drives were straightened to improve traffic flow. The bridge's popular name, referring to the famous triumphal arch erected in London's Hyde Park in 1851, is a misnomer, as the structure was actually built of white limestone quarried in nearby Westchester County.

to carriage drives because it is hardly thought that any plan would be popular in New York, that did not allow of a continuous promenade along the line of the drives, so that pedestrians may have ample opportunity to look at the equipages and their inmates." In any event, the outspoken opposition of commissioners Robert Dillon and August Belmont, the avid horseman and Rothschild agent, to the whole and particulars of the Greensward plan forced Olmsted and Vaux to entirely recast their initial circulation plan in response to Belmont's request, sustained by the full board, that an extensive bridle path be added to the park.

This revision introduced the principle of "separation of ways" for all three classes of traffic within the park, and though it may initially have rankled, the complication of the bridle path led Olmsted and Vaux to more fully exploit the long-established principle of the designer guiding movement through the landscape. The visitor, no longer bidden to cross drives or the bridle path at grade, was relieved of potential danger. Just as importantly from the designers' standpoint, a more varied and also more nuanced experience could now be crafted, as the stroller was now easily led through a controlled sequence of vistas by way of the felicitous proliferation of bridges and archways that, with Bethesda Terrace, were to become the park's chief architectural adornments.

The original Greensward plan projected nine bridges, most to be built of wood, but to implement the separation of ways Vaux designed nineteen remarkably varied spans between 1859 and 1865. By 1872, there were thirty-four bridges in the park with two others yet to be constructed; eventually three other rustic stone bridges were added to the Upper West Side of the park in the 1890s, necessitated by the settling of the upper reaches of Central Park West. The park's bridges were originally numbered in order of the

Above: The original Gapstow Bridge was built in 1874 to span the northern neck of the Pond and was a unique design—a wooden segmental arch bridge supported by masonry abutments and detailed with oversized, decorative iron bosses suggesting Victorian-era industrialism. In 1896, severely weakened, it was replaced by a graceful arch built of Manhattan schist (pp. 108–109). The photograph documents the bridge shortly before its removal, reinforced with triangular wooden bracing and a second deck. Two electric pontoon boats silently ply the Pond's waters.

Above: Calvert Vaux's gouache rendering of Denesmouth Arch, among his earliest bridge designs. Completed in 1860, the bridge carries the 65th Street Transverse Road and spans a major footpath linking the Dene and the Central Park Zoo. Built of pale, olive-hued New Brunswick sandstone, the bridge originally sported bronze lamp standards crowning its piers and revetments, long ago removed in response to repeated vandalism.

Following pages: Diminutive Dipway Arch is faced with pale grey granite ashlar from Rackliff Island, Maine, and carries Park Drive over the pedestrian path linking Heckscher Playground and the Carousel. Authors' watercolor.

commencement of their construction, though in 1873 Olmsted prescribed them anglicizing names, with *bridge* designating a structure spanning water and *arch* indicating a span across land. However, like a romance language, there are several exceptions to these rules, the most notable being bridge 28, named *a posteriori* Gothic Bridge (*pp. 120–121*). Since this much-admired bridge spans the bridle path, it should correctly be named Gothic Arch.

While three of the most beautiful and significant arches in the lower park—Spur Rock (*p. 122*), Outset and Marble (*p. 123*)—fell casualty to land takings and the dubious imperative of improved traffic flow, mercifully the better part of Vaux's bridges not only remain in situ but also have been restored to their former glory. All were constructed to the highest standards, and together they catalog a rich variety of designs and materials, from rustic log bridges to highly refined cast-iron, brick and ashlar masonry spans.

Of all the park's bridges, the most innovative and distinctive are its seven cast-iron spans, five of which remain. To contemporaries, these bridges were a revelation; they were judged both æsthetic and technological marvels and were lauded by architects, engineers and the public of the day and gained Vaux an international reputation. As a group, they are distinguished by an elegant balance between delicate detailing and bold purity of line. Mould, who oversaw their ornamentation, characteristically detailed their balustrades with a delicate, repeating tracery melding overlapping geometrical figures with foliate arabesques. Their taut, flattened aches echo the elegant limestone spans designed by the graduates of France's renowned academy of civil engineering, the École des Ponts et Chaussées, who had brought the science of stereotomy (vaulting with stone) to a high art. Vaux fused the characteristically long, flat vault of the French bridge with the delicacy of Mould's cast-iron tracery, creating spans at once bold and delicate. These

bridges were at the forefront of technological developments and employed cast iron and steel with daring and innovation. In fact, with the exception of a bridge in Brownsville, Pennsylvania, the cast-iron bridges that Vaux designed for Central Park are the earliest such spans erected in the United States.

Unlike their predecessors in English landscape parks or French Anglo-Chinese folly gardens, the bridges of Central Park are sited as inconspicuously as possible, with the conspicuous exception of Bow Bridge (*pp. 114–115, 117, 118*), justly ranked among the park's most famous structures. Excepting the rustic Ramble Arch (*opposite*), the stone bridges in the lower half of the park are formal designs with smooth-faced ashlar predominating, occasionally banded with brick. In contrast, the park's northern reaches feature several rustic stone bridges—most notably Huddlestone Arch (*p. 131*), composed of massive, dry-laid boulders—that meld perfectly with their woodland setting.

The designers had agreed from the outset that all architectural elements introduced into the park be subordinate to nature, deriving their character from and enhancing the landscape in which they were set. As we have already noted, the original Greensward plan foresaw but a handful of bridges for a park of exceptional extent, almost all of which

Above: The vaulted interior of Glen Span Arch, traversing the Loch and featuring arched grottoes. Originally a wooden span carried on stone pilings, the bridge was rebuilt in the 1880s with rusticated gneiss ashlar. Photograph by Cornelis Verwaal.

Opposite: Vaux's picturesque and diminutive Ramble Arch stands in its namesake, the Ramble, a densely wooded hill north of the Lake. The massive boulders flanking the arch were moved to the site to heighten the setting's drama. Photograph by Andrew Zega.

Above: Calvert Vaux's original design for bridge 22, a rustic wooden footbridge erected in 1861 to span the spur linking the Lake to Ladies' Pond, an intimately scaled, barbell-shaped pond nestled just inside the park's western border between 75th Street and Manhattan Square. The pond, drained and filled in the 1930s to provide a neighborhood playground, was so named because it was reserved for women's skating in the winter months. Authors' watercolor.

Left: An engraved view from 1869 depicting the footbridge in its final form, with heavy transverse logs and buttresses added to the balustrades. Balcony Bridge appears in the distance.

Above: Huddlestone Arch, built of massive boulders set without mortar, carries vehicular traffic over the Loch. Erected in 1866 to a design attributed to Calvert Vaux, the arch's rustic construction embodies the wilderness æsthetic employed in landscaping the northernmost reaches of the park. This design shift was largely a cost-saving measure but also a fortuitous one, for the contrast to the pastoral landscaping of the lower park adds unexpected variety and richness to the visitor's experience. The bridge is found at the base of a rugged, wooded escarpment that drops steeply toward the Harlem Meer, which—at 14 feet above sea level— is the lowest point in Central Park. Authors' watercolor.

were to be fashioned of rough logs, a rustic style (to be examined in the following chapter) that the partners believed would be as unobtrusive as possible and which they adopted as the default architectural vocabulary for the myriad minor structures necessary to furnish a major urban park: summerhouses, gazebos, shelters, arbors, small footbridges, benches—even the park regulations were posted in a rustic, log-framed display case.

A Sentimental Education

Clearly, the designers initially had seriously underestimated the complexity of the park's circulation routes and the number, scale and durability of the bridges necessary for them. The addition of the bridle path drove this point forcefully home. Moreover, Olmsted and Vaux were opposed by a wealthy and powerful faction hostile to their vision, while the majority of the park board and the public were primarily interested in obtaining a pleasant and well-equipped pleasure ground, whatever its ultimate form. Above all, Vaux's magnificent bridges addressed these sentiments; they also offered Olmsted his first major lessons in accommodating his pastoral ideals to the realities of park-making in a major city. Two fundamental precepts were unavoidable: First, the public not only desired major architectural set pieces in a large park, it considered them a necessity. Second, architecture is essential to park-making and provides an elemental contrast between the man-made object and the naturalistic setting which enhances both. A pastoral landscape, no matter how artfully crafted, will ultimately be judged wanting if unrelieved by signs of man's intervention.

Olmsted's early ideals and vision would lead him to obsessive quests for perfection out of all keeping with the wider responsibilities of his position, most notably at the Ramble, where he planted and replanted, seeking an elusive perfection reminiscent of Louis XIV's manic, decades-long quest for the perfect carp basins at Marly. No king, he met his match when confronted with the fanatical penury of comptroller Andrew Green and was simply ignored as irrelevant by the Sweeny board. These experiences seasoned him: they hardened his resolve, tempered his idealism and broadened his perspectives. Olmsted did truly breathtaking things—shaping the face of America's cities—as a result.

VIII RUSTIC SHELTERS

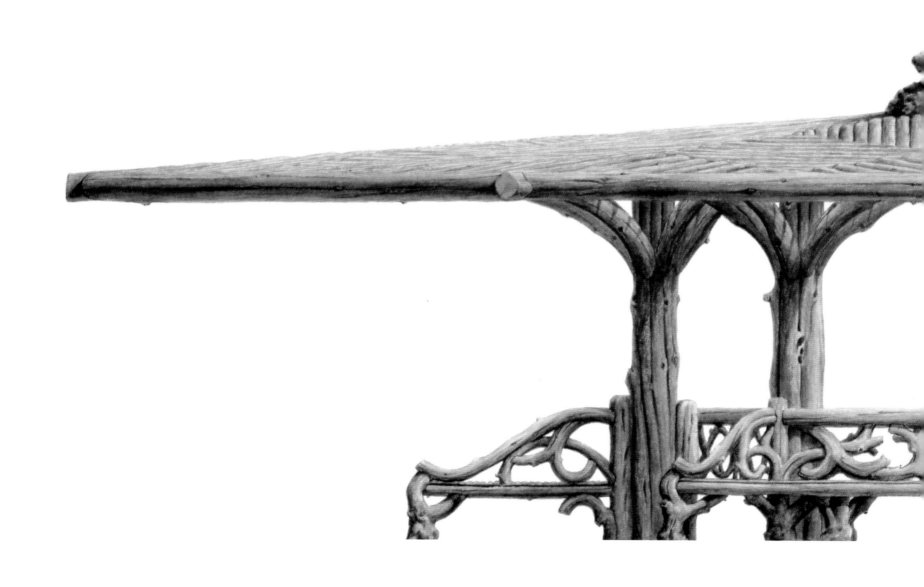

*There is scarcely a prettier or more pleasant object for the
termination of a long walk in the pleasure-grounds or park,
than a neatly thatched structure of rustic work, with its
seat for repose, and a view of the landscape beyond.*

Andrew Jackson Downing, 1849

CENTRAL PARK BORE WITNESS to rustic architecture's first great flowering in America, delineated through the rich variety of picturesque cedar-log structures that Calvert Vaux designed there. Though frontier cabins were still common throughout rural areas, few direct precedents for this remarkable burst of creativity are to be found on American soil, and even fewer in American writings of the period. A great deal of credit has rightly been given to Vaux's partner Andrew Jackson Downing, who published designs for rustic structures in his books and in the *Horticulturist*. His Highland Gardens estate featured rustic log seats and shelters embowered in leafy alcoves as well as a rustic pavilion he named the Hermitage, all doubtless inspired by similar covered rustic seats and a lake-side pavilion at Montgomery Place—a venerable Dutchess County estate which had impressed him deeply and which became his æsthetic lodestar. Upon his death in 1852, Downing's influence was already immense, though today it is often reduced to a simplistic carpenter-Gothic domesticity embodied by his talisman, the vine-clad front porch. Vaux's stunningly ingenious confections of split and peeled logs, gnarled boles, tortured roots and knotted burls are a silent tribute to Downing's genius and in turn Montgomery Place's hold on Downing's imagination.

Intellectual Currents

Vaux was an Englishman by birth, a perceptive æsthete and wily intellectual, practicing his art in a self-consciously picturesque age. In 1856, the preeminent æsthete of that age, John Ruskin, published volumes three and four of his monumental *Modern Painters,* examining Nature through the prism of art and art through morality and spirituality. Among his discourses, Ruskin analyzed the character and depiction of trees at great length (*p. 136*), and devoted the entirety of volume four to alpine landscapes. Here, Ruskin, a deeply religious man torn between the rule of intellect and the power of emotion—and ultimately between reason and faith—was intellectualizing and dissecting the components of the Sublime, an ancient concept he astutely linked to the grotesque.

Ruskin built on the foundations of Rousseau, and Vaux—unavoidably influenced by Ruskin (as was a generation; Olmsted would cite him from memory)—divined a renascent flowering of the rustic, picturesque vocabulary of thatched hermitages, gnarled garden seats and living, espaliered bowers that had been a staple of English and European gardening for centuries, melding that inspiration with Downing's precedents to create his masterful log structures. They were widely admired by contemporaries and architects remarked them nearly as often as they cited Vaux's bridges for praise, and these rustic structures—far more numerous in the early park than they are today—were a potent means of conjuring the spirit of picturesque romanticism both partners worked so tirelessly to impart to the park's design. Ironically, though, this rustic-grotesque æsthetic was intended to evoke the very "pathetic fallacy" that Ruskin had criticized at such length: the style's tortured logs and high romanticism begged an emotional response—the selfsame emotions which, Ruskin observed, misguided artists were attributing to an indifferent Nature.

Preceding pages: An elevation of a long-destroyed "rustic summer-house" built to overlook the Ramble, Lake and Belvedere from Cherry Hill. The structure's nearly flat, open-beamed patchwork roof is a remarkable interpretation of the low-pitched, sheltering roofs of traditional Swiss chalet architecture. Authors' watercolor.

Opposite: An engraving from 1869 depicting the Cherry Hill summer-house, whose novel roof suggests a massive wooden parasol.

Above: Arbor in the Ramble with Terrace in the Distance. Lithograph by G. W. Fasel, 1862.

Clarence Cook, who did not depart from his class's reflexive prejudice against immigrants (he incongruously described Vaux as "an Englishman by birth and training" while he prefaced effusive praise of Olmsted by calling him "an American of Americans"), wrote extensively of Central Park's rustic structures and praised them highly. He attributed much of their impetus to "a certain Hungarian," apparently referring to Anton Gerster, a Hungarian immigrant who maintained a long association with Olmsted and Vaux and who carried out much of the actual construction of these structures:

> The summerhouse near the Artists' Gate [Cop Cot, which still stands] is one of the very earliest erected in the Park. Those first built were designed by a certain Hungarian, who showed a great aptitude for this kind of architecture at least, and who was ably seconded by the workmen the Commissioners employed to assist him. Hardly any thing of the sort had ever been seen before in this country, but since that day a great many, almost as good in design, have been put up in various parts of the Park by other hands. The material employed is the common cedar, which so abounds in the vicinity of New York. The limbs and trunks are stripped of their bark, and they are then put together in a solid and workmanlike fashion, very unlike the frail and flimsy structures which we commonly meet with under the name of summerhouses.

Decades later, Vaux's rustic æsthetic was to mature into a truly American vernacular style, expressed as the Adirondack and Great Lakes camp styles, and eventually it would be adopted as the semiofficial architectural vocabulary of the nascent National Park Service.

Opposite, above: The Park Bench *by William Merritt Chase, 1890.*

Opposite, below: Strength of Old Pine, *lithograph after John Ruskin,* Modern Painters, *Vol. IV, 1856.*

Above: A Currier & Ives sleigh ride through Central Park, photographed from behind a rustic, Chinese Chippendale balustrade by George P. Hall & Son, 1906.

Of course nothing is ever truly new under the sun, and the precocious French elite, under Jean-Jacques Rousseau's liberating influence, had been erecting rustic wood garden follies during the reign of Louis XV in the mid-eighteenth century. As if to prove his influence to posterity, Rousseau himself died in a rustic, thatch-roofed hermit's hut in the gardens of Ermenonville in 1778. And to cite but two examples of his legacy, in 1771 royal architect Jacques-Germain Soufflot designed "the Origins of Architecture," a rustic wood interpretation of a Greek temple, for the Marquis de Marigny's estate of Ménars (*p. 138*). Marigny, director of royal buildings, rejected Soufflot's project, but in 1780 the architect Jean Chalgrin erected a dairy constructed of brick and tufa and fronted by a pedimented temple portico fashioned of bark-clad logs for the Comtesse de Province in the town of Versailles.

The Cherry Hill Summerhouse

The watercolor that opens this chapter is based upon a construction drawing dated July 27, 1866, detailing a rustic summerhouse that once stood on Cherry Hill not far to the west of Bethesda Terrace. Though the building is long destroyed, the drawing documents the hexagonally planned shelter's construction with a cutaway section and roof plan that details a honeycomb pattern of infill logs. The curious *gloriette* supports its flat, exaggeratedly cantilevered roof with a ring of mature tree trunks, as if the shelter grew from the earth itself. The flat, open roof is a remarkably abstracted interpretation of the low-pitched, sheltering roofs so characteristic of Tyrolean chalet architecture.

Such was the versatility of Vaux's rustic style that it could effortlessly transform a Chinoiserie garden folly into a delightful garden arbor (*p. 141*). Regrettably, this simple kiosk—built on a hexagonal plan, its flaring roof carried by six rough-hewn logs—was a

minor embellishment that has been irrevocably effaced. Nonetheless, its innocent grace renders it a particularly charming eye-catcher and a rare witness to the era of the park's inception, known only from a stereoptic view. From its stick-work lattice walls to its crowning *orbis mundi*, reinterpreted as an acorn-shaped bole, the pavilion is a whimsically naïve homage to the myriad garden kiosks built throughout Europe in the eighteenth century.

If for a moment we imagine that garden bridges are literally able to transverse moods and sensibilities and indeed time itself, then exotic follies such as this would be their destination. Such a simple fantasy, like a waking dream, became a point of departure for a voyage of the spirit, evoking foreign cultures and distant lands at a time when crossing Manhattan to visit the park was itself a serious journey—Olmsted in particular was deeply concerned with encouraging working-class families to visit the park and providing a healthful and enriching experience for them. The pavilion was a distant echo of the opulent diversions of a distant, aristocratic age, democratized by its rusticity to suit a people's park.

The Dene Shelter

The Dene Shelter offers unobstructed views from an impressive rock outcrop near Fifth Avenue and 68th Street, and few more perfect spots can be found to contemplate Manhattan on a summer's day. Today backed by the screen of Fifth Avenue's imposing apartment blocks, the rustic belvedere overlooks its namesake, the Dene, a gently sloping valley running south toward the Zoo. The shelter is reached from a winding trail terminating in steps cut from the living bedrock and, with the Cop Cot pavilion to the west of the Pond, is one of the few large, rustic log structures remaining in the park. Ingeniously, Olmsted and Vaux perched these picturesque pavilions atop rock outcrops that otherwise would have detracted from their æsthetic vision. The shelter's plan is actually quite formal, recalling Renaissance *tempietti*—a central octagon crowned by a clerestory and flanked by apsidal wings. After a recent restoration, the shingled roof depicted in the watercolor has been removed and the openwork roof beams exposed.

Above: The Origins of Architecture, an unrealized project by Jacques-Germain Soufflot for the gardens of the Loire Valley estate of Ménars, 1771. Authors' watercolor.

Opposite: The Dene Shelter near Fifth Avenue and 68th Street, seen in end elevation. The pavilion's shingled roof was removed during a recent restoration. Authors' watercolor.

Above: The Wisteria Pergola, completed in 1863 to designs by Olmsted and Vaux. Today, the 130-foot-long pergola still tops a promontory to the east of the Concert Ground and Bandstand. Stereoptic view, circa 1870.

Left: The spectacular octagonal Children's Summer House, or Kinderberg, built in 1866 to designs by Vaux and located south of the 66th Street Transverse Road, today site of the Chess and Checkers House. Stereoptic view, circa 1870.

Opposite: A small hexagonal pavilion melding rustic and Chinoiserie elements, circa 1865. This minor structure is known only through a stereoptic view, and its former location is unknown. Authors' watercolor.

On the whole he's quite handsome, if one looks at him rightly.

Hans Christian Andersen, *The Ugly Duckling*

MONG THE MISCELLANEOUS EXPENSES authorized by the park's board of commissioners for January 1867 were $6 for spittoons, $46 to Olmsted, Vaux & Co. for drafting work, $80 for badges (which was $2.75 more than was spent on legal services the month prior) and $15 to one A. H. Gallatin for a monkey. The odd primate found amid tallies of nails, paint, lumber and gravel, though it does give one pause, nonetheless succinctly encapsulates the haphazard genesis of the Central Park Zoo.

That same month, Olmsted and Vaux had drafted a memorandum proposing that a large zoo be constructed at Manhattan Square on the park's west side (today site of the American Museum of Natural History), but the letter was received by the board with little enthusiasm. Like the conservatory and to a lesser extent the natural history museum, a zoo was one of the park's orphaned children, understood by all as a necessity but lacking a committed constituency. While the Vanderbilts, Marquands, Taylors and Morgans of the world were keenly investing vertiginous sums in the glamorous pursuit of artistic philanthropy, camels, elephants and kangaroos were more beloved of the common man and offered no serious competition to Rembrandts, Vermeers and Fragonards. Olmsted and Vaux advised and drew plans which were duly considered; discussions were held and letters written, but nothing concrete—excepting the purchase of a leopard or antelope now and again—ever came of these periodic, desultory motions.

With dark poetic justice, the Arsenal—the universally loathed eyesore which critic Clarence Cook dismissed as "a flimsy, make-believe structure [lacking any] useful purpose"—served as a storehouse for "somewhat incongruous 'gifts'" to the city, and its basement became a pound for cast-off animals, while the largest were ranged in makeshift pens on its lawn. Though the porcupines, owls, parrots, foxes and the occasional alligator or coatimundi were dutifully tallied in the appendices of the commission's annual reports with the same Victorian punctiliousness given the explication of the year's drainage and sewerage work, this makeshift arrangement lingered on for well over a decade, slowly gaining more and more interesting animals as well as an interested public, until things came to a head when Boss Tweed's Tammany Hall regime swept briefly into power in 1870–1871, sending Olmsted, Vaux and the Stebbins board into exile and lofting Jacob Wrey Mould to a moment of supremacy over the construction of Central Park.

Among Mould's many perceived transgressions during his day in the sun was having the temerity to design a wooden Menagerie building which was erected beside the Arsenal (which he also inexplicably renovated), ignoring Olmsted and Vaux's moribund proposition that the largest zoological park in the country was to be built at Manhattan Square with nonexistent funds at some indefinite date in the future. Though makeshift, Mould's Menagerie was wildly popular with the public and received more than two and

Preceding page: The Honey Bear, a bronze fountain *by Brooklyn native Frederick G. R. Roth, installed at the Central Park Zoo in 1937. Authors' watercolor.*

Opposite, above: The Arsenal and the Menagerie in the late nineteenth century. The zoo, which Olmsted and Vaux originally intended to occupy the site of the American Museum of Natural History, grew haphazardly from a collection of cast-off animals housed in the Arsenal's basement and in makeshift outdoor pens.

Opposite, below: The Menagerie building, a wooden pavilion, was designed by Mould as a temporary zoo structure and erected in 1871 on the grounds of the Arsenal.

a half million visitors in 1873—well over a quarter of all park entries—severely muting criticism from his newly reinstated superiors. Despite the Menagerie's enormous popularity, successive administrations followed a policy of benign neglect and occasional hostility to its continued existence. As late as 1890, Olmsted—who could by then recall a dozen failed schemes for a zoo—remarked that there was no "portion of the Park that is more crowded, or in which the people, and especially the children find more amusement." However, he admonished, "the leading purpose of the Park is not the amusement of the People."

In 1895, a group of wealthy Republican sportsmen, among them the city's chief police commissioner, Theodore Roosevelt, won state approval to create an extensive, state-of-the-art zoological park, the future Bronx Zoo, to be controlled by a private board. Yet such was the depth of popular sentiment for the nine acres of Central Park's Menagerie that the bill authorizing the creation of the Zoological Society could not be passed until an amendment was voted ensuring the Menagerie's continued protection.

Robert Moses and the Central Park Zoo
The Central Park Menagerie attracted three million visitors in 1902, far more than the city's museums and the newly opened and vastly larger Bronx Zoo, yet it received a paltry operating budget, ensuring that it slipped into dilapidation and disrepair. Paradoxically, the Great Depression gave the zoo new life under the reform administration of Parks Commissioner Robert Moses, who moved to rebuild the compound with characteristic alacrity. Within a year of taking office, Moses, using an army of Works Progress Administration laborers paid with Federal relief funds, saw to it that the Menagerie's ramshackle sheds were razed and a modern, brick-and-concrete zoo was erected (*p. 150*). The rectangular compound, its pavilions centered about an open plaza dominated by the iconic sea lion pool, was an enormous success, and Moses and his WPA army then turned

Opposite: The larger-than-life-size bronze statue of the heroic Alaskan sled dog Balto stands atop a naturalistic bedrock outcrop near Willowdell Arch at the level of 67ᵗʰ Street on the park's east side. Authors' watercolor.

Above: Balto and musher Gunnar Kaasen, who led the final legs of the famed Nome "diphtheria run" of January 1925, at the sculpture's dedication in Central Park that same December.

to reshape the park for active recreation, to the delight of the public but to the increasing disquiet of preservationists.

A progressive and a reformer, Moses remarked on several occasions that Central Park was "essentially a playground," and he ensured that it boasted them in abundance. He augmented the venerable Heckscher Playground with twenty-two satellites, seventeen of which were "marginal playgrounds" built near the park's borders and intended for neighborhood use. He also transformed Olmsted and Vaux's open meadows furnishing "healthful recreation" with baseball diamonds, football fields, tennis and volleyball courts, croquet lawns, horseshoe pitches and of course courts for his beloved shuffleboard.

Throughout his remarkably uncontested and unprecedentedly autocratic reign, Moses remade Central Park, rationalizing, standardizing, straightening, paving, maintaining, regulating and policing it into an optimized product of progressive administration. Because he was universally acknowledged to be incorruptible and above petty politics, as well as effective and fair-minded, he and his policies garnered deep—indeed near-universal—support. Working-class New Yorkers hailed Moses for his tireless efforts to expand access to recreation while also improving its quality and variety. Even Mayor La Guardia was impressed. "No law, no regulation, no budget stops Bob Moses from his appointed task," he once remarked.

Moses and the Children

Among the many initiatives Moses pursued to ensure that Central Park became more accessible and enjoyable to the public was his touching insistence that new sculpture for the park bring joy to the city's children. Moses would have no more of Victorian pedagogy: gone were the dour, forgotten statesmen and brooding, minor poets which even Olmsted and Vaux had not succeeded in banishing from the park's grounds. In their place Moses welcomed the superb animal sculptures of Frederick G. R. Roth, famed author of *Balto*, whose works, such as *The Honey Bear* fountain (p. 143), embellished the rebuilt Central Park Zoo, as well as the lyrical bronzes of Paul Manship, who sculpted the bronze gates of the original Children's Zoo and Osborn Playground, the gnomon of the Waldo Hutchins Bench (p. 167) and *Group of Bears*, sculpted in 1960 but erected posthumously in 1990 at the playground at Fifth Avenue and 79th Street, to the immediate south of the Metropolitan Museum of Art.

Likewise, a children's storytelling area, originally proposed for the English or Secret Garden at Conservatory Garden, was established during the Moses administration just to the north of Conservatory Water (p. 111) and features the popular sculptures of *Hans Christian Andersen and the Ugly Duckling* by Georg Lober (pp. 154, 155), commissioned to mark the 150th anniversary of the Danish author's birth and dedicated in 1956, and *Alice in Wonderland* (1959) by the Catalan sculptor José de Creeft.

Balto

The bright golden polish upon this larger-than-life-size bronze, a result of the clambering of generations of children, is physical proof that *Balto* is among the most beloved sculptures in Central Park. The statue commemorates the famous Siberian husky that led the final two legs of a heroic sled relay from Nenana to Nome, Alaska, in January 1925,

Opposite: A detail of Frederick G. R. Roth's Balto, *for which he was awarded the 1925 Speyer Prize by the National Academy of Design. Among the most popular sculptures in the park, the bronze portrait of the world-famous sled dog is burnished by the touch of countless visitors' hands. Authors' watercolor.*

delivering a precious cargo of diphtheria antitoxin to the isolated city's threatened residents. The developing drama captured the world's attention as the territory's governor organized an emergency sled relay to transport the serum to the otherwise inaccessible city. Traversing the 670-mile distance by sled would have required well over three weeks under normal circumstances, yet the relay teams completed the run in little more than five days, despite braving blizzard conditions and temperatures of -50° Fahrenheit.

Balto, who had never before led a team, safely guided his master Gunnar Kaasen and a team of seven dogs through an Arctic blizzard on the final two legs of the relay, thereby saving untold lives. Kaasen remarked, "I couldn't see the trail. I gave Balto, my lead dog, his head and trusted him... It was Balto who led the way. The credit is his." The event transfixed the world; even today, two restaurants are named after Balto in Paris, France. After a period of crass exploitation, the dogs were rescued by the citizens of Cleveland, Ohio, and lived out their days at the Cleveland Zoo.

Balto stands on a rough-hewn bedrock outcrop near Willowdell Arch at the level of 67th Street, blending seamlessly with its naturalistic plinth. Frederick G. R. Roth executed *Balto* in 1925; the National Academy of Design awarded him the Speyer Prize for the work that same year. Roth trained at the Academy of Fine Arts, Vienna, the Royal Academy,

Above: An aerial perspective of the 1934 Central Park Zoo, its brick-and-concrete pavilions arranged about a central courtyard featuring the sea lion pool, overlooked by the crenellated Arsenal at right. The zoo was rebuilt from 1983 to 1988 after the designs of Kevin Roche John Dinkeloo and Associates and is now operated by the Wildlife Conservation Society. Drawing by T. Kautzky.

150

Berlin, and the New York Academy and worked in the tradition of French animaliers, nineteenth-century sculptors who specialized in the realistic depiction of animals. *Balto* is universally recognized as the masterwork of a long, distinguished career.

The Delacorte Musical Clock

Set atop a brick arcade dividing the precincts of the Central Park Zoo from the Children's Zoo, the whimsical Delacorte Musical Clock (*p. 153*) enchants children of all ages with its unlikely band of a concertina-playing elephant, a fiddling hippopotamus, a drumming penguin, a horn-playing kangaroo, a piping goat and a tambourine-tapping bear. When a pair of mallet-toting monkeys peal the clock's crowning bell every hour and half-hour, they set the musical menagerie twirling to one of forty-four nursery rhymes and seasonal songs.

Inspired by the elaborate automata benefactor George T. Delacorte had admired in Europe, the clock was designed by Edward Coe Embury—son of Aymar Embury II, the chief architect of the 1934 zoo—in collaboration with designer Fernando Texidor. The Italian sculptor Andrea Spadini executed the animal figures. Dedicated in 1965, the clock has since become a beloved park fixture, and its complex mechanisms are checked daily to ensure that the much-anticipated display unfolds, as they say, like clockwork.

*Opposite: The Ugly Duckling
immortalized in bronze.
Authors' watercolor.*

*Above: The seated bronze of
Hans Christian Andersen by
Georg Lober was installed near
Conservatory Water in 1956.
Photograph by Ed Yourdon.*

X MEMORIALS AND MONUMENTS

First-rate statues are as yet hardly to be got for money here,
though we cordially believe that they will be produced in good
time; but until they can be had it is best to wait, for a second-
rate statue is like a tolerable egg—it is not to be endured.

Clarence C. Cook, *A Description of the New York Central Park*, 1869

THE MAGNIFICENT GILT-BRONZE equestrian statue of General William Tecumseh Sherman is the centerpiece of Central Park's official entrance at Grand Army Plaza at Fifth Avenue and 60th Street. Dedicated in 1903, it is the last major work of the celebrated Irish-American sculptor, Augustus Saint-Gaudens, over which he labored for nearly a decade, and is unanimously considered his masterwork. The goddess Nike, brandishing a palm frond, symbol of triumph, leads the general south toward glory, with his striding horse and flowing cape adding palpable momentum to the sweeping composition.

Though not set in the park proper, the sculpture acts as the park's monumental gateway, following the board of commissioners' dictum that the park was "to be enjoyed not only on reaching particular places or centers, but at the very entrance." Sherman's March to the Sea (symbolized by a sprig of Georgia pine being crushed beneath his mount's hoof) sealed Union victory in the Civil War and was his foremost military accomplishment, but his unflinching strategy of total war, disregarding any human or economic expense, perturbs his fame and foreshadowed the horrors of modern warfare.

Begun in 1858, the park's construction was largely completed by 1864, in the midst of the Civil War. The area below 102nd Street was fully open to the public and carriages by the end of 1863, the same year when the park's four northernmost blocks, from 106th to 110th streets, were finally acquired after a four-year delay. The 65-acre parcel brought the park's final area to 843 acres. Attention then turned to properly defining the park's boundary with the city. The park's borders and main gates were seen as the culmination to a triumphant construction campaign, but the question of their materials and form became mired in an economic, æsthetic, political and class battle set off by the machinations of Richard Morris Hunt.

The Uninvited Guest

Hunt was the first American architect to study at the École des Beaux-Arts in Paris and, besides his talent, had the brilliant foresight to launch his career by being born to the influential Hunt family of Vermont. Then in his late thirties, the architect stood at the cusp of an illustrious career to be crowned by commissions for the main façade of the Metropolitan Museum of Art and the pedestal of the Statue of Liberty. Born of society, he was already a prominent society architect, designing Loire Valley châteaux on Fifth Avenue and in Newport for Marquands, Vanderbilts, Belmonts and Astors (p. 33).

With Olmsted in self-imposed exile in California and Vaux reduced to an unpaid consultant's position after both had resigned in May of 1863 to protest comptroller Andrew H. Green's usurpations, Hunt's brother-in-law and Central Park commissioner, Charles H. Russell, induced the rump board to approve his designs for four elaborate

Preceding page: The goddess Nike, clutching a palm frond symbolizing victory, guides Sherman to glory. Saint-Gaudens' muse for the figure was Harriette "Hettie" Anderson, a young African-American woman from South Carolina who the sculptor described as "certainly the handsomest model I have ever seen." Authors' watercolor.

Opposite: The Sherman Monument at Grand Army Plaza, Augustus Saint-Gaudens' masterpiece, stands upon a pink granite socle designed by architect Charles McKim. The sculptor despised statues resembling "smoke stacks" and ordered the work finished with two layers of gold leaf. Photograph by Hasan Ahmed.

Beaux-Arts entrance plazas where Fifth to Eighth avenues met the southern border of the park. Quite naturally, Hunt described his designs as "elegant and appropriate" mediators between the city fabric and the park, and an ally promoted them in the *New York Post* (with no mean rhetorical flourish, even for a florid age) as a method to transform the park into "one great open air gallery of Art, instead of being, as some dreamers fancy it, a silent sketch of a rural landscape caught up and enclosed within the raging tumult of a vast metropolis."

Hunt's design for the park's main entrance at Fifth Avenue and 59th Street (*opposite*) is a distillation of the grandiloquent Parisian urbanism of Napoleon III. The composition is anchored by a central fountain-*cum*-roundabout and features a pair of equestrian statues raised on high pedestals framing the park's entrance—an overt citation of the famed *Chevaux de Marly* at the Place de la Concorde, though only two monumental statues had been judged sufficient to mark the origin point of the Champs-Élysées, not six. Crammed mere yards away, in a reflexive, École de Beaux-Arts-instilled horror vacui,

Above: A sweeping view north along Fifth Avenue circa 1920, with the newly completed Grand Army Plaza, designed by Carrère & Hastings, in the foreground. Above is the Sherman Monument, below it the Pulitzer Fountain, designed by the sculptor Karl Bitter and dedicated in 1916. Note the Hotel Netherland, the dark building at right, demolished in 1926 to make way for the Sherry-Netherland Hotel (p. 37).

Above: A drawing by Richard Morris Hunt depicting his proposal for a grandiose Beaux-Arts plaza at the park's main entrance at Fifth Avenue and 59th Street, one of four to face the avenues abutting Central Park South. Hunt's scheme, initially adopted due to his brother-in-law's influence, was ultimately rejected as inappropriate and excessively costly. Note the copy of the Louvre occupying the site of the Plaza Hotel.

is an overwrought ensemble—a raised exedra featuring a commemorative column, a grotto *and* flanking cascades—that terminates the inconsequential 60th Street cross axis. *La pièce de résistance,* a transplanted Louvre occupies the site of the Plaza Hotel.

Comptroller Green considered the Greensward plan a quasi-sacred vision and so was little disposed toward Hunt's grandiose and costly plazas. As he had assumed the day-to-day oversight of the park's construction and (grudgingly) paid its bills, he deferred their execution in favor of completing the Harlem annex. Green's temporization allowed Vaux, who had also cultivated a coterie of wealthy and influential New Yorkers, to mount a countercampaign against Hunt's project. Playing upon egalitarian sentiments, Vaux likened Hunt's plazas to the antechambers of Versailles: "The imperial style presumes that people wait, wait and hang around, and provision is made for clients, courtiers, subordinates and laqueyes [sic]" to cool their heels in suitable splendor. New Yorkers had no need of such airs, he proclaimed. "How fine it would be to have no gates" at all, and "to keep open House and trust all always."

161

Hunt's scheme, doomed as much by its cost as by its fundamental clash with the park's æsthetic vision, was eventually shuffled aside and the question of the form of the park's enclosure then came to the fore. Several commissioners admired the fences enclosing Parisian parks, but Olmsted, citing Ruskin, remarked that "An iron railing always means thieves outside or Bedlam inside." Despite the expense, Vaux persuaded the board to approve a low stone wall. Today, these rusticated brownstone boundary walls, cast green with moss, are as comfortingly familiar to New Yorkers as chrome yellow taxis.

With consummate taste, Hunt died in 1895 in Newport, amid the resplendent Gilded Age "cottages" he had designed. Three years later, the Municipal Art Society (which Hunt had cofounded, as he had [with Vaux] the American Institute of Architects), commissioned his memorial from the architect Bruce Price and sculptor Daniel Chester French. Price cast the monument (*above*) as an elaborated, elongated exedra supporting a screen of Ionic columns. The architect's portrait bust, raised on a pedestal, is framed by an abstracted portico crowned by an outsized anthemion, symbol of classical architecture. Life-size female bronzes, allegories of Painting and Architecture, bracket the composition.

The William T. Stead Memorial

The decorous William T. Stead Memorial honors the life and career of the revered English editor, investigative journalist and champion of social justice. Stead, who had been widely expected to receive a Nobel Prize that same year, died on the *Titanic* in 1912 but displayed stoic integrity by helping women and children into lifeboats and offering his life jacket to another passenger. He was last seen clinging to flotsam beside John Jacob Astor IV.

Above: The Richard Morris Hunt Memorial, a Beaux-Arts exedra commemorating the renowned Gilded Age architect, is sculpted of white Vermont granite from his native state and features bronzes by Daniel Chester French, best known for his seated figure of Abraham Lincoln at the Lincoln Memorial in Washington, D.C.

Opposite: The William T. Stead Memorial, a bronze bas-relief plaque dedicated to the memory of the crusading English journalist who died on the Titanic. *Photograph by Bernd H. Dams.*

Following pages: Fortitude (left) and Sympathy (right), diminutive bronzes from the William T. Stead Memorial. Authors' watercolors.

The bronze bas-relief plaque (*above*) was designed by the renowned New York firm of Carrère & Hastings, architects of the New York Public Library, and is set into the park's boundary wall just north of Engineers' Gate at 91st Street and Fifth Avenue, facing the Cooper-Hewitt Museum and sheltered beneath a large street elm. The British sculptor George J. Frampton executed the work, a restrained, poetic monument evoking chivalry and charity. A pair of diminutive sculptures, a medieval knight representing Fortitude and an angel depicting Sympathy, flank Stead's profile portrait, framed by a garland of laurels, symbolizing glory and achievement.

FORTITVDE

The Waldo Hutchins Bench

Nestled in a small clearing just north of 72nd Street and Fifth Avenue, the Waldo Hutchins Bench offers fine views of Conservatory Water. Built in 1932 of pale rose granite, the bench honors an original member of the park's board who subsequently served twice as parks commissioner and three terms as a member of Congress. Like the Richard Morris Hunt Memorial some yards away, the memorial takes the elegant form of a classical exedra, a *demilune* exterior bench. Often inset into niches and sheltered by colonnades, exedræ naturally fostered conversation and thus came to symbolize Greek philosophy. In time, the form was codified in the Roman basilica, a public tribune where magistrates sat in a *demilune* niche at one end of a rectangular hall. The basilican plan was also adapted for religious buildings, with the exedra reserved for the altar, and thus the form is a powerful and multifaceted symbol: the literal seat of philosophy, justice and divinity. Classically inspired exedræ were a favorite ornament in eighteenth-century English landscape gardens and were seen as the perfect spot from which to contemplate an Arcadian landscape, preferably one with a Greek temple folly set in the distance.

While its graceful lines and impressive mass project dignity and serenity, the bench's formality is leavened by its decorative details—notably the pair of crisply carved bas-reliefs of squirrels (*p. 4*) which embellish its arms, lighthearted symbols of Central Park wreathed in glory. A Latin inscription, graphically incised across the bench's back, reads *Alteri Vivas Oportet Sit Vis Tibi Vivere* (One lives by living for others).

Below: The Waldo Hutchins Bench was designed by Eric Gugler and executed by Corrado Novani and the Piccirilli brothers, who also worked on the Lincoln Memorial in Washington, D.C., and the USS Maine Monument. Photograph by Bernd H. Dams.

Opposite: This delicately detailed sundial was designed by Albert Stewart and is centered behind the bench's back. The bronze gnomon of a lyrically abstracted female dancer was sculpted by Paul Manship. The Latin inscription reads Ne Diruat Fuga Temporium *(May time's passage not destroy). Authors' watercolor.*

Strawberry Fields

Yoko Ono, John Lennon's widow, conceived Strawberry Fields as a living memorial to her slain husband and dedicated the site on what would have been the singer's forty-fifth birthday, October 9, 1985. The two-and-a-half-acre informal garden occupies a sloping triangle of land at Central Park West and 72ⁿᵈ Street near the Dakota Apartments, the family's residence and the site where Lennon was murdered on the evening of December 8, 1980. Ono worked with landscape architect Bruce Kelly and the Conservancy to transform the parcel into a Garden of Peace with plants donated by over 120 nations.

The iconic *Imagine* mosaic, a simple round set in the pavement at the heart of the garden, has become a shrine to Lennon's memory, collecting notes, flowers and votive candles from his myriad fans, and it is the site of annual vigils to celebrate his birth and mourn his death. Though often described as interpreting traditional Roman patterns, the design is actually far more expressive than this reading allows and alludes to Lennon's uniquely provocative pacifism and strongly Buddhist leanings and worldview. IMAGINE, the title of Lennon's famous 1971 peace anthem, holds the center of an abstracted lotus flower made of thirty-two radiating segments, the number of Buddha's virtues. In Buddhist traditions, the fully opened lotus, rising above muddied waters, symbolizes enlightenment, and a white lotus connotes purity of mind and spirit. The duality of black and white represents matter and spirit, the mud from which the lotus blooms and the blossom of understanding. And finally, the flower signifies rebirth in a figural and literal sense, entirely appropriate to honor a musician who integrated Buddhist mantras into his music and Buddhist philosophy and a Buddhist worldview into his life.

Disarmingly simple, a single word centering an abstracted flower, Lennon's memorial owes an enormous conceptual debt to Maya Lin's revolutionary 1982 Vietnam Veterans Memorial in Washington, D.C., which overturned traditional notions of a monument's form and conceptual underpinnings. However, the mosaic takes Lin's abstraction a step further by renouncing three-dimensionality entirely and setting its single-word message into the earth, where it can be trod upon or reverenced—a wry and profoundly insightful evocation of Lennon's humanity and spirit.

The Gates

A monument's defining characteristic is its longevity, enduring across time to reach from the past to the present, thus informing the future. Transience is therefore the monument's principal foe. The Bulgarian artist Christo and his wife Jeanne-Claude rose to international fame by subverting this very idea with a series of spectacular, ephemeral environmental artworks employing fabric in innovative and provocative ways. *The Gates*, a monumental installation, stood in the park during sixteen days in February 2005, the culmination of twenty-five years of planning. More than 7,500 metal gates hung with bright saffron orange fabric panels straddled twenty-three miles of pedestrian paths, the billowing fabric and intense color standing in charged contrast to the wintry bleakness of the park. That *The Gates* was temporary was essential to its realization: permanence was unthinkable. Provocative, monumental, visionary, poetic and ephemeral, *The Gates* defies easy categorization or definition, but its æsthetic impact and visual grandeur revealed Christo's desire not only to dazzle with the strange beauty of his art but also to unsettle with the shock of the improbable and the fantastic made real. Christo remade Central Park into his personal dreamscape and invited the public to walk its sinuous paths and inhabit his vision. Demounted, that vision imprints itself upon the memory, with the park becoming the installation's memorial.

Opposite, above: The famed Imagine *mosaic in Strawberry Fields was executed by Italian craftsmen and donated by the city of Naples. The memorial to John Lennon is among the park's most visited attractions.*

Opposite, below: The Altar to Reverie at Ermenonville, a French landscape garden renowned for objects inscribed with aphorisms, such as this invocation "To Dream." Authors' watercolor.

Above: A view of The Gates *with* The Falconer, *a bronze by George Blackall Simonds, in the foreground. Photograph by Cornelis Verwaal.*

Its fields are bountiful and provide for each day.
Its granaries overflow, they reach the sky.
Its ponds teem with fish and its lakes with birds.
Its fields are green with grass and its banks bear dates.
He who lives there is happy, and the poor man is like the great elsewhere.

Beloved Country, an ancient Egyptian poem

THE EGYPTIAN OBELISK is Western society's most potent and coveted talisman and literally stands as the physical marker of civilization itself. Of the twenty-one ancient obelisks standing today, Egypt itself retains only four; Rome is graced by thirteen, all plundered by its emperors, then reerected during the Renaissance. The Victorians, who coveted them as profoundly as had the Caesars, raised the remainder in Istanbul, Florence, Paris, London and New York. Why this is so is obvious, for obelisks are quite simply the perfect monument: They are rare in the extreme, they were conceived as sacred monuments by the semidivine rulers of the world's greatest ancient civilization, and they are the largest, heaviest and most elegant objects ever crafted by man.

Objects of Awe

All ancient obelisks are monoliths quarried from the fine pink granite found at Aswan, ancient Selene, located on the banks of the Nile in Lower Egypt. The earliest obelisks were raised at On, the sacred ceremonial city known to us today by its Greek name, Heliopolis, city of the sun, or more exactly, city of the sun god Ra. Obelisks were always erected in pairs in the temple forecourt, flanking the pylon—a massive, chamfered wall pierced by a central portal that gave access to the inner courtyard.

In form, an obelisk is defined by a square-sectioned, tapering shaft and a pyramidal cap, known logically enough as the pyramidion. Like the classical Greek columnar orders (i.e., Doric, Ionic and Corinthian), obelisks follow certain proportional rules: The height of the shaft ranges from nine to eleven times the width of the base, and the pyramidion's height equals the width of the base. The largest obelisks are—excepting the extraordinary foundation stones at Baalbek, Lebanon—also the largest monoliths ever created. Like the Greeks did with classical columns, Egyptian masons employed entasis—an imperceptible, convex bulging—to give the long shaft a pleasing visual equilibrium.

Obelisks were invariably carved with hieroglyphs celebrating the pharaohs commissioning them. Pyramidions were, as today seen on the Luxor obelisk at the Place de la Concorde in Paris, capped with gold ("the flesh of the gods"), and many obelisks were entirely sheathed in polished copper sheets or, more rarely, with iron or entirely with gold, evoking the golden phallus of the mythical first pharaoh, Osiris.

"Cleopatra's Needle"

At 71 feet tall and weighing 244 tons, the Central Park obelisk, commonly known as Cleopatra's Needle, was one of a pair originally erected before the temple of the sun at On for Pharaoh Thutmosis III in 1443 B.C. Some two centuries later, Ramesses II ordered its flanks carved with hieroglyphs commemorating his military victories. With

Page 171: The pyramidion and upper shaft of the Central Park obelisk, or "Cleopatra's Needle," which stands near the Metropolitan Museum of Art. Detail of the authors' watercolor reproduced on page 177.

Above: The obelisk being demounted in Alexandria, Egypt, under the direction of Navy Lt. Commander Henry H. Gorringe in 1880.

Right: The obelisk's transport was a complex and delicate undertaking: 112 days alone were required to traverse the west side of Manhattan from the Hudson River to the site at Greywacke Knoll. Thousands gathered to witness its reerection on January 22, 1881.

the collapse of dynastic Egypt and the abandonment of On, the obelisks, long toppled, were reerected by the Roman prefect Pontius at Alexandria before the Caesarium during the reign of Emperor Augustus in 12 B.C. Already worn by time, the obelisk's base was stabilized by bronze rods at each corner, dissimulated by sculptures of crabs.

With the opening of the Suez Canal in 1869, a group of influential New Yorkers led by William H. Hurlbert, editor of *The New York World*, and backed by the rail magnate William H. Vanderbilt, began to militate that the United States be offered the "gift" of an Egyptian obelisk. Their case of European obelisk envy only intensified in 1877, when the English engineer John Dixon undertook the removal of the fallen Alexandrian obelisk—a gift to England dating from 1819 in gratitude for Lord Nelson's victory over the French in the Battle of the Nile. (After a near-disastrous sea voyage, the obelisk was erected at Victoria Embankment, London, in 1878.)

Dixon, sensing a profit to be made, informed Hurlbert that he could demount and ship the remaining obelisk from Alexandria to New York for the sum of £15,000. Vanderbilt avidly assented, but the deal foundered when Khedive Ismail Pasha indicated that the obelisk in question was not Dixon's to sell and that any negotiations were to be undertaken by the government of the United States and not with private parties. Unperturbed,

Above: The firm of Kevin Roche John Dinkeloo and Associates, the successor firm to Finnish modernist Eero Saarinen, was engaged as master planner of the Metropolitan Museum of Art in 1967. Roche designed six massive additions to the museum, constructed from 1975 to 1990. This dramatic glass curtain wall shelters the Michael C. Rockefeller galleries of African and Oceanic art. The Met's incursions into the park were met with stiff opposition and marked the end of the museum's physical expansion. Photograph by Bernd H. Dams.

174

Above: The obelisk and the early Met in a more genteel age. Calvert Vaux and Jacob Wrey Mould designed the original art museum in a Ruskinian Gothic style, and an initial section was opened in 1880, meeting with stiff criticism from museum trustees. Theodore Weston, engineer and museum trustee, designed the southern wing in the late 1880s, photographed here in 1893. This Victorian core was subsumed by subsequent additions authored by Richard Morris Hunt, McKim, Mead & White and Kevin Roche John Dinkeloo and Associates.

Hurlbert arranged negotiations through the offices of the State Department. Talks dragged on through the winter, but the Khedive eventually relented, consenting to the obelisk's removal in May of 1878.

After a year's planning, the obelisk's arduous, yearlong transport was supervised by Lieutenant Commander Henry Gorringe, a U.S. Navy engineer. Once lowered by fulcrum—with a heart-stopping, uncontrolled drop that thankfully did no damage—the obelisk was slid into the hold of the dry-docked steamer *Dessoug* through an opening in its hull. Seven months were required to lay temporary lumber tracks and winch the obelisk across Manhattan to Greywacke Knoll behind the Metropolitan Museum of Art where, with great pomp, ceremony and speechifying, it was reerected upon its original base on January 22, 1881, in the presence of Secretary of State William Evarts and a crowd of 10,000 extremely chilled spectators.

The obelisk's saga created a press frenzy, and more than 9,000 Freemasons had already paraded up Fifth Avenue simply to celebrate laying the cornerstone of its plinth on October 2, 1880. However, before any heated editorial battles over appropriate sites could commence, a self-appointed site selection committee—Hurlbert, Gorringe and the landscape painter Frederic Church, enlisted in an effort to paper over the fait accompli—announced its decision rubber-stamping Vanderbilt's inscrutable and ill-advised choice

of a site, which essentially reduced the obelisk to the status of a lawn ornament in the Museum's backyard—a narrow strip of turf backed by the eastern flank of the old Receiving Reservoir. Vanderbilt, owner of the New York Central Railroad (with its notoriously murderous Manhattan tunnel), was then the world's richest man and a major donor to the Museum. He would achieve lasting and well-deserved infamy for uttering "The public be damned!" the following year.

That Vanderbilt determined the obelisk's placement was a gross abuse of influence, but this outrage would hardly have mattered if the site he had selected had not resulted in the greatest squandered opportunity for civic embellishment in the city's history. With breathtaking hubris, Gorringe stated flatly, "In order to avoid needless discussion of the subject, it was decided to maintain the strictest secrecy as to the location determined on." He then listed Greywacke Knoll's advantages: Its "isolation"—a perfectly absurd requirement for a major public monument—its elevated prospect and the site's underlying bedrock, which ensured a firmly anchored foundation, lest Manhattan suffer "some violent convulsion of nature."

Indeed.

Above: A view of the obelisk looking east toward Fifth Avenue in the 1890s with the southwestern corner of the Metropolitan Museum of Art at left.

Opposite: The east face of the Central Park obelisk in elevation. The hieroglyphs incised on the obelisk's flanks commemorate Ramesses II; only the pyramidion bears traces of inscriptions lauding its commissioner, Thutmosis III. Authors' watercolor.

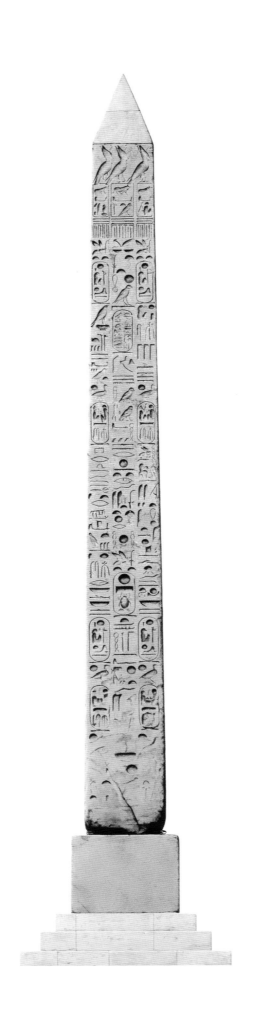

XII THE USS *MAINE* MONUMENT

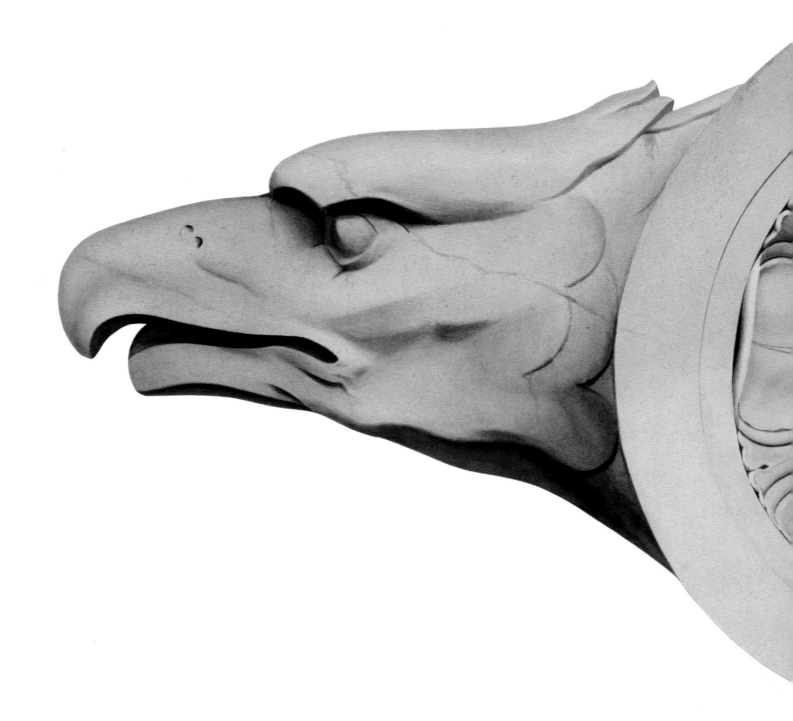

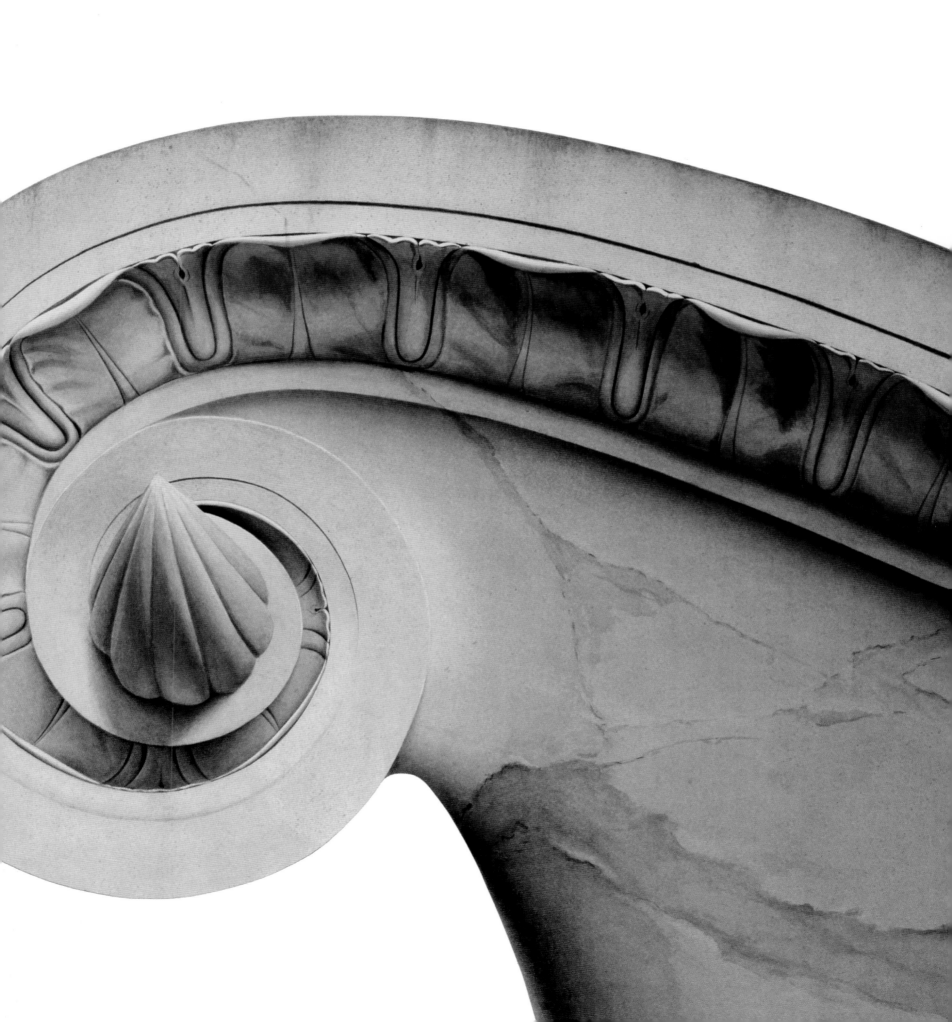

Remember the Maine! To Hell with Spain!

Rallying cry of the Spanish-American War

THE USS *MAINE* was the US Navy's second pre-dreadnought battleship (after the USS *Texas*); these warships were the first in the American fleet to dispense with the full masts of Civil War–era ironclads and rely entirely on advanced, coal-fed steam boilers for propulsion. The ships were constructed in response to the alarming naval might of Brazil, which had commissioned several battleships from Europe, most notably the imposing *Riachuelo*, delivered in 1883. As a result, Brazil stood unchallenged as the dominant naval power in the Americas in the 1880s.

The *Maine* and the *Texas* were the first modern warships built in the United States, at a time when the country lacked sufficient technological prowess and industrial infrastructure to bring such an ambitious project quickly to fruition. Construction dragged on for nine years (three years alone were spent waiting for the armor plate), and the ship was finally commissioned in 1895, entering active service the year following.

With nearly fifteen years between conception and service, the *Maine* was flagrantly obsolete upon delivery. Its en echelon main guns, cantilevered over the hull, had already been found ineffective by European navies years before it had entered service; its ramming bow was a quaint leftover from a prior epoch of naval warfare dating back to Roman triremes; its heavy armor had been superseded by innovative lightweight armor; and it had neither the firepower to face true battleships nor the speed to serve as an effective cruiser. In short, the *Maine* was both a white elephant and a sitting duck.

The Sinking of the Maine

In January of 1898, less than two years after entering active service, the *Maine* was ordered to Havana Harbor as a show of American might during the Cuban War of Independence. Weeks later, on the evening of February 15, a massive explosion devastated the forward third of the ship and the *Maine* sank within moments, taking with it 266 crewmen. The foreship, torn by the massive explosion, sank nearly instantaneously; the stern, where the captain's cabin was located, settled more slowly. Neighboring ships immediately launched rescue parties to search for survivors. "Chief among them," Captain Charles Sigsbee later noted, "were the boats from the *Alfonso XII*. The Spanish officers and crews did all that humanity and gallantry could compass."

The actual cause of the sinking of the *Maine* has remained a mystery despite an initial Naval inquiry held in 1898 and a second in 1911, after the *Maine's* wreck had been cofferdammed and forensic and salvage operations completed. The dead were buried with honors at Arlington and the hulk was scuttled at sea. After reviewing these reports, Admiral Hyman Rickover initiated a private investigation in 1974. Though his team brought advanced forensic tools to bear, his report agreed with the second board

Preceding pages: The allegorical prow of the USS Maine Monument depicted in elevation. Authors' watercolor.

Above: The battleship USS Maine depicted in a lithograph reproducing the painting of Fred Pansing, 1900.

of inquiry, concluding that the *Maine* was destroyed not by a Spanish mine or bomb but by the detonation of the forward powder magazines. Rickover posited the spontaneous combustion of highly volatile bituminous coal (which the Navy had recently adopted, replacing slower- and cleaner-burning—and far less dangerous but more expensive—anthracite coal) in the bunker abutting the forward gunpowder magazine. A spark or heat from the coal fire traversed the bulkhead, igniting the gunpowder and dooming the ship.

Yellow Journalism and American Expansionism
Of course, this forensic science was carried out far too late to check William Randolph Hearst and Joseph Pulitzer, who were locked in a frenzied war for domination of New York's lucrative daily newspaper market. The infamous era of corrupt, manipulated, exaggerated and patently false reporting known as yellow journalism reached its sordid nadir with frenzied dispatches detailing nonexistent cannibalism, torture and atrocities committed by Spain against Cuba—all in an effort to drag the United States into war against Spain in a bout of newfound American expansionist brinkmanship.

Hearst managed to eclipse even Pulitzer in ruthlessness, and he infamously sent his star delineator, Frederic Remington, to Havana to document Spanish atrocities. After several uneventful weeks, Remington cabled Hearst, "There is no war. Request to be recalled." Hearst replied, "Please remain. You furnish the pictures, I'll furnish the war."

Opposite: The USS Maine *Monument soon after its dedication in 1913. The main sculpture group is entitled* The Antebellum State of Mind: Courage Awaiting the Flight of Peace and Fortitude Supporting the Feeble.

Right: The main sculpture group, executed in Tennessee pink marble. The boy is intended to hold aloft a pair of bronze wreaths, often stolen, symbolizing victory. The woman behind him embodies Peace, flanked by Courage, left, and Fortitude, right. Photograph by Lissette Carrera.

Hearst was true to his word. In the weeks following the *Maine* disaster, his flagship paper, the *New York Journal*, speculated wildly about Spanish duplicity under a relentless onslaught of banner headlines. Pulitzer rivaled Hearst in warmongering (though he stated privately that "nobody outside a lunatic asylum" believed the Spanish had sabotaged the *Maine*). Lesser editors were also not to be underestimated in their jingoism, and together the yellow press stoked war fervor with editorials demanding both vengeance for the sinking of the *Maine* and the defense of American honor. The rest, as they say, is history.

The Monument
The USS *Maine* Monument was also a Hearst publicity vehicle, just as the Spanish-American War had been "his" war, and he browbeat *Journal* readers with an equally relentless subscription campaign. In response, more than a million Americans donated funds to erect the memorial—an overwhelming outpouring of sentiment that should have humbled and shamed Hearst (but did not), since his newspaper empire had made enough blood profit by promoting and then reporting upon the United States' Caribbean adventure to underwrite war memorials across the nation.

However, it soon became apparent that, despite the constant fund-raising publicity, no one in the Hearst empire had actually bothered to secure a site for the memorial. In consequence, the proposed monument was ignominiously rejected from one location after another until finally it was accepted for the Merchant's Gate of Central Park, facing Columbus Circle at Central Park South.

The site was far from ideal, as the monument competed for attention with the rostral column and basin centering the roundabout already dedicated to Christopher Columbus, engendering an awkward surfeit of commemoration in a city whose relentless grid and equally relentless property speculation ensured that it was otherwise largely bereft of civic embellishment. Olmsted and Vaux had decried and defended against just such depredations upon the park's integrity for decades, arguing persuasively that Central Park was not a catchall repository for monuments, sculpture and public institutions but rather that such structures should be judiciously dispersed throughout the city, thereby enriching its neighborhoods while maintaining the park's integrity.

Ideally, the monument's Beaux-Arts formalism, as well as its ambition and scale, demanded that it be erected on its own plaza and set on an axial alignment with the city's street grid. Siting it on a truncated wedge of parkland diagonal to, and thus in conflict with, two major thoroughfares was a monumental planning blunder only surpassed by the absurd location of the obelisk. In both cases New York's leading figures, operating without the perceived impediment of public scrutiny and on an ad hoc basis, failed miserably to rise above self-interest and half-measures to ensure that major civic projects were successfully realized in their totality. Instead, they honored posterity by erecting magnificent but appallingly sited monuments to squandered opportunity. The affront is redoubled when one first considers that two major thoroughfares—Central Park South and Central Park West—terminate at Columbus Circle. When one adds the obvious observation that the USS *Maine* Monument was conceived to terminate just such an axis but instead was wedged between two of them and imbricated in the park's greenery, the failure is complete.

Opposite: Columbia Triumphant, *the gilded bronze sculpture group crowning the USS* Maine *Monument, reputedly cast from bronze cannon recovered from the Maine's wreckage. Authors' watercolor.*

The Design

The monument itself was designed by architect Harold Van Buren Magonigle, a student of Calvert Vaux and a former apprentice in the august offices of McKim, Mead & White. An accomplished artist and sculptor, Magonigle employed these gifts in his architectural work to great success, and his artistic sensibilities led him to excel in designing the Beaux-Arts monuments for which he is best known. He also authored the McKinley Memorial in Canton, Ohio, and the Liberty Memorial in Kansas City, Missouri, though the USS *Maine* Monument ranks as his most elegant and successful design.

Magonigle anchored the composition with a massive, chamfered pylon of Maine granite enriched with a Roman Doric entablature. The simple form evokes ancient Egyptian temple architecture and provides an austere backdrop for the sculpture ringing its base. The pylon's faces are detailed with trapezoidal frames, and the names of the dead are engraved on the panels on its flanks. The highly accomplished suite of allegorical sculptures embellishing the scheme were conceived by Magonigle and executed by Attillo Piccirilli and his atelier. Piccirilli was an Italian stonemason and master carver who emigrated to New York City from the famed Carrara quarries in Tuscany, whereupon he and his sons dominated the execution of sculptural stonework in the city for decades.

Above: The USS Maine *Monument was dedicated on May 30, 1913, with ceremonies honoring the ship's lost seamen conducted by President William Howard Taft and Spanish-American War veterans.*

Opposite: The Michelangelesque Atlantic Ocean, *one of a pair of reclining allegorical figures flanking the base of the monument. Its pendant depicts the Pacific, the war's other maritime theater. Authors' watercolor.*

The gilded bronze sculpture group atop the pylon, *Columbia Triumphant (p. 185)*, is unfortunately difficult to view from street level—yet another failing of the memorial's site. Nonetheless, it is superbly conceived and masterfully executed, and it was reputedly cast from bronze recovered from the *Maine*'s own main batteries. The chariot group shares an ancient lineage with the *Quadriga of Victory* crowning Berlin's Brandenburg Gate and the *Triumphal Quadriga* of St. Mark's Basilica, Venice, a tradition with roots in Imperial Rome. The quadriga was the four-horse Roman chariot raced at circuses and hippo-dromes throughout the empire, and these chariots came to symbolize victory, conquest and fame, often with Minerva, goddess of war, at the reins. The *Maine*'s eagle's head prow *(pp. 178–179)* is remarkable in that it encapsulates and predates the æsthetics of art moderne by decades. The other sculptures are of equal quality, and none have a hint of the saccharine or the substandard about them, either in conception or execution.

In all, the USS *Maine* Monument is masterfully executed, though today we seem to have become inured to the dignity, grace and measure of the Beaux-Arts æsthetic. Hidden in plain sight, the memorial has relative obscurity due to its inexplicable siting, a deficiency it also shares with the Central Park obelisk, thus ranking both as the most overlooked and underappreciated monuments enriching the heart of Manhattan.

XIII BUILDINGS AND PROJECTS

Nature first 2nd and 3rd—architecture after a while.

Calvert Vaux, 1865

FREDERICK LAW OLMSTED AND CALVERT VAUX nourished a pastoral, Arcadian vision for Central Park, a legacy of Rousseau's belief that communion with Nature edifies and ennobles man's spirit, enriched by their shared intention, shaped by republican convictions, that the park should serve all the people. Both were fundamentally opposed to a formal design mimicking the Parisian parks of the Tuileries or Luxembourg gardens and championed by powerful factions who saw the park as an extension of the city rather than an oasis from it, and though they were worldly enough to recognize that a major urban park demanded a great number and variety of built structures—a park without a conservatory would have been unthinkable; a large ornamental lake likewise demanded a boathouse—they fought with tenacity those encroachments they viewed as inimical to that vision. They steadfastly maintained that the park's overriding purpose was to provide relief from the "overwrought" atmosphere of city life, and that siting monuments and public institutions elsewhere would greatly benefit the city and its populace. Indeed, Vaux wrote Olmsted, "we are the final guardians of this interest as long as we live."

Thankfully, the partners were most often successful, perhaps not so much due to their eloquence or even the power of their arguments but to the hard fact that the park's commissioners understood the simple truth that trees, grass, rocks and water are much less expensive than buildings and fine monuments. When the practical need was justified, then Vaux, often seconded by Mould, designed these structures with great care, paying particular attention to the overall scenic effect such an addition would play in the park.

Thomas Hastings' 1890 design for a tool house that opens this chapter (*pp. 188–189*) is a testament to Vaux's enduring creative relevance. Hastings, then thirty, was principal in the fledgling firm of Carrère & Hastings, which would later rival Richard Morris Hunt in garnering prestigious commissions, chief among them that for the New York Public Library in 1897. However, such projects lay years in the future, and Hastings was then a staff architect for the city's Department of Public Parks, a post earlier held by Jacob Wrey Mould. Hastings reprised Vaux's design for the Thatched Shelter built in Prospect Park, Brooklyn, circa 1867 (*opposite*), polishing and condensing the scheme and upgrading its log walls and thatched roof—the same picturesque/grotesque vocabulary Vaux employed so successfully in the rustic log structures discussed previously—to stone and cedar shingles, transforming a lowly tool shed into an appealing fieldstone cottage. Two diminutive turrets of rock-face ashlar frame a large, arched driveway and are capped by sinuous, bell-shaped roofs evoking rural English vernacular architecture. Despite ashlar masonry and a cedar-shake roof, the folly projects a remarkable winsomeness, though doubtless the expense of those materials led to the scheme's abandonment.

Above: A stereoptic view of the Thatched Shelter or "Swiss Thatched Cottage" in Prospect Park, Brooklyn, designed by Calvert Vaux in 1867. The structure was destroyed by fire in 1937.

Unquestionably, the most unexpected structure apparently erected in the park was a diminutive, rustic-Chinoiserie belvedere (p. 192) discovered among hundreds of stereoptic views of park features. This wooden trifle, perched on a massive outcrop like those which Olmsted spent such efforts to conceal, is a moment of scenographic genius—and may well have been authored by Mould in wry homage to the hundreds of colorful pagodas erected in the Anglo-Chinese folly gardens of late eighteenth-century Europe (p. 193).

The enduring European fascination with the Chinoiserie style is often misunderstood; these gaudily painted stick-and-lathe pagodas, perched on artfully composed rockwork grottoes, were never intended to be faithful interpretations of authentic Chinese architecture; rather, they were a means to evoke the Orient and its fascinating mysteries, but more fundamentally they were a means to liberate the fantasy—an aristocrat's playhouse. As the craze waned and the shock of the French Revolution remade Europe, Chinoiseries fell from favor, symbols of aristocratic indulgence. However, by the mid-nineteenth century, with the passage of barely two generations, these charming garden houses reemerged, testifying to their irresistible appeal.

The pagoda was designed on a pentagonal footprint, the unusual shape entirely appropriate for such an eccentric belvedere, and a further note of whimsy is added by sheltering

191

it beneath a witch's-hat roof. And just as the peaks of eighteenth-century pagodas were often crowned with pagodas in miniature in a kind of fractal redoubling, so the upper roof is ringed with toylike reductions evoking birdhouses. The pavilion's rustic log construction curiously accentuates its fragility, yet another element of its appeal and doubtless the reason for the brevity of its charmed existence.

The Ladies' Pavilion

If Vaux's series of elegant cast-iron bridge designs for the park's carriage traffic and pedestrians were remarkably innovative, then Mould's Ladies' Pavilion (*p. 195*) is the exact mirror of its era. Constructed in 1871 of wrought and cast iron, Victorian building materials par excellence, the shelter originally stood at Central Park West and 59th Street.

In 1912, the shelter was displaced by the USS *Maine* Monument and relocated to the scenic outcropping at Hernshead, overlooking the Lake near West Drive at 75th Street. Standing on a stone plinth, the pavilion commands sweeping vistas across the Lake, though its filigree ornament, a fanciful amalgam of Gothic and Tudor details, clashes unavoidably with the area's rustic character. Sixteen slender cast-iron colonnettes originally supported a polychrome slate roof crowned by a delicate, cast-iron ridge crest. The

Opposite: This wry, rustic homage to the late eighteenth century's craze for Chinoiserie pagodas was perched atop a massive stone outcrop and is known only by this stereoptic view attributed to Central Park. If true, the backdrop of evergreens suggests a location near the former Maze.

Above: The pagoda at Bonnelles, an Anglo-Chinese folly garden built circa 1780 for the duc d'Uzes. The pagoda-belvedere, focus of an elaborate ensemble, stood atop a large artificial rockwork dominating an artificial lake and was reached by a series of rustic, arching footbridges. Engraving by Georges Le Rouge.

restored pavilion is a small Victorian gem, decorously facing Bow Bridge across the Lake, a reminder of an era when practicality did not preclude beauty.

The Casino

One of the original specifications of the park's board was a music hall to be sited east of the Mall. With the completion of the Old Bandstand on the Mall proper (*p. 39*), that condition was met and the project for the site near Fifth Avenue and 72nd Street was recast as the Ladies' Refreshment Salon, a restaurant built in 1864 after designs by Calvert Vaux that permitted unchaperoned women to dine in propriety. In time, such notions were considered archaic and the concession was renovated; the newly renamed Casino (*p. 198*), decorous and genteel, became the park's main restaurant, and in summer months it extended its service to offer light meals and refreshments in the Arcade beneath Bethesda Terrace (*p. 75*). The Casino's exterior more resembled a sedate summer cottage than a public building, but its sumptuous interiors assured a wealthy clientele— also engendering a steady stream of criticism. By the close of World War I, the Casino had again fallen from favor, described by *Variety* as "a somewhat dumpy nightclub," but that was destined to change dramatically with the ascendancy of "Gentleman Jimmy" Walker.

Mayor Walker incarnated the Roaring Twenties. A charismatic former crooner and man-about-town much appreciated by mobsters, Walker bewitched the city's electorate with a dashing lifestyle and populist posturing and was elected mayor in 1926. He promised to complete the park's stagnant renovation during his campaign, and once in office saw to it that the Casino, an old watering hole, regained its former glory. City lawyers annulled its lease and the concession fell to a Walker intimate who, backed by a board whose wealth and influence were doubtless the envy of the Metropolitan Museum of Art, set the Viennese architect Joseph Urban to remake the property into a sophisticated nightclub. Urban, a stage designer for the Metropolitan Opera, created the legendary ballroom, clad in smoke-black mirrors etched with art deco tulips, seating 600 guests.

Inaugurated the fourth of June in the inauspicious year of 1929, the Casino became an instant—though short-lived—fixture of Manhattan nightlife. It was said, barely in jest, that the mayor ran the city from a corner table. Dubbed "the high hat hut," the Casino's reputation soared when "G-men" raided it within months of opening. That October's Wall Street crash saw the fortunes of the Casino's patrons erased and Walker's own fortunes sour. In the ensuing panic, the mayor came to incarnate the decadent excesses popularly believed to have caused the crash, just as he had earlier embodied the glamour and optimism of the Jazz Age. Governor Franklin D. Roosevelt, eyeing the White House, launched an investigation that revealed breathtaking municipal corruption, forcing Walker to resign in 1932 and flee to Paris with his mistress, a showgirl from the Ziegfeld Follies.

Above: "Cares and business and the work-a-day world vanish when you enter there." An 1895 magazine illustration of Scholars' Gate, the main entrance to Central Park at Fifth Avenue and 59th Street, depicted eight years before the area was redesigned as Grand Army Plaza. A passenger shelter, similar to the Ladies' Pavilion seen opposite, appears at left.

Opposite: The Ladies' Pavilion, a cast-iron shelter designed by Jacob Wrey Mould, was demounted and moved to Hernshead in 1912 to make way for the USS Maine Monument. The watercolor depicts Mould's initial design for a polychrome slate roof. Authors' watercolor.

194

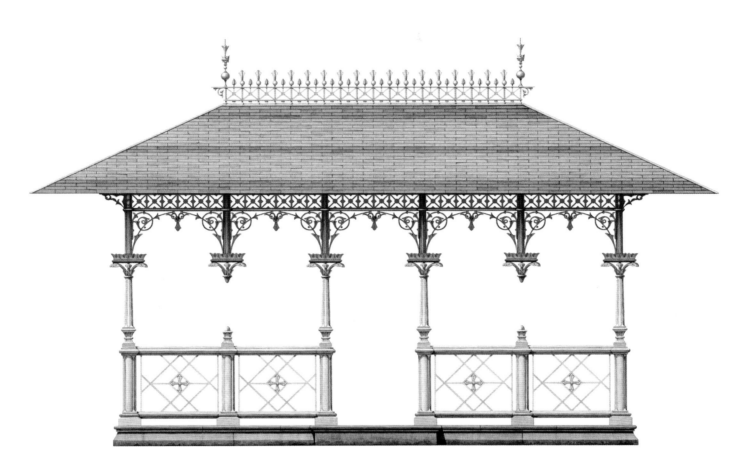

In 1934, at the depths of the Great Depression, the new park commissioner, Robert Moses—who despised "that whoopee joint" as a symbol of Walker's corruption, remarking that a meal there was more expensive than dinner at the Plaza Hotel—ordered the Casino demolished with Mayor Fiorello La Guardia's blessing. With laconic understatement, *The New York Times* observed that the Casino "had never been noted for catering to the poor." Moses commissioned the Rumsey playground for the site, and since 1990 SummerStage has offered free musical concerts there—finally fulfilling the first park board's vision for a music ground at that location.

The Forgotten Children
After their tumultuous resignations during the Civil War, Olmsted and Vaux were reappointed to their positions in July 1865, but two months after the end of hostilities, opening a new era of park expansion and consolidation. During the war, the city's press had strongly criticized the lack of children's amenities in the park, and to redress this oversight the park commissioners designated much of the area south of the Mall as a children's district. The precinct was bounded to the east by the Arsenal and the existing, albeit ad hoc Menagerie (*p. 145*), to which Olmsted and Vaux added the Kinderberg or Children's Pavilion (*p. 140*), the Carousel, the Dairy and the Boys' and Girls' playhouses, today greatly augmented by the Central Park Zoo, Wollman Memorial Rink, Heckscher Playground and the Chess and Checkers House, built on the site of the Kinderberg in 1952.

In 1887, an aging Vaux, whose fortunes had diminished in inverse proportion to the ascension of his former partner Olmsted, returned to the Department of Public Parks as a landscape architect. That year, Mayor Abram Hewitt had passed the Small Parks Act; Vaux designed a number of pocket parks about the city in response and in 1891 prepared plans for a children's playhouse for Central Park (p. 199), cast in the shingle style then ubiquitous in such summer resorts as Newport and the Hamptons. Intended to straddle the 65th Street Transverse Road defining the northern border of the children's precinct, the innovative design would have been the park's only hybrid bridge, its steel-arched substructure reprising his own elegant Terrace Bridge, built in Prospect Park, Brooklyn, in 1890. Hybrid bridges first appeared in English landscape gardens, most famously Sir John Vanbrugh's aptly named Grand Bridge in Blenheim Palace park, completed circa 1708. Such structures were foremost garden follies and eye-catchers, built to span artificial lakes or picturesque streams, and were crowned by small pavilions, temples or pagodas. Vaux brought this idea to its intriguing conclusion, the bridge becoming the very structure it supported.

Above: The marble bar of the Mineral Water Pavilion, or Spa, distant progenitor of today's corporate-sponsored arenas, whose construction cost was underwritten by Carl H. Shultz, owner of a successful mineral water company. The grandiose indoor fountain dispensed "selzers-water, the chief remedy in Asiatic cholera, the very milk of our mother earth" to park visitors, chief among them German Jewish immigrants who took the waters in the morning while the Schultz band played outside.

Above: The festive Mineral Water Pavilion stood near the Green and was designed by Vaux and Mould on a Latin cross plan. Styled as a Moorish fantasy evoking the opulence of Europe's great spa resorts, the piebald Spa, like the Old Bandstand nearby, was a garden folly in the truest sense. By the 1920s soda and snacks had displaced mineral waters, and the pavilion was demolished in 1957.

The Dairy

Near to the Carousel, the Dairy (p. 200) was built in 1870 after Vaux's designs but was completed as a restaurant under Mould's supervision during Vaux's short-lived exile under the Sweeny board, though Vaux promptly restored it to its intended purpose upon his return in November of 1871. Though not a component of the original Greensward plan, the building was conceived to provide fresh milk to children visiting the park, in pointed response to a series of horrific midcentury "swill milk scandals." In the late 1840s, unscrupulous dairymen began diluting the city's milk with water, then adding flour, chalk or plaster to restore its consistency. In Brooklyn dairies, cows were fed alcoholic mash, the leavings from the whiskey distillation process. By the late 1850s, infant mortality had tripled, and nearly 8,000 city children died annually from toxic dairy products and cholera. Reform laws passed by the state legislature in 1862 ended these unspeakable practices and the model Dairy was promoted as a symbol of restored faith in the integrity of New York's milk supply. On February 18, 1870, *The New York Times* reported:

The Commissioners of the Central Park have determined to erect and open next Spring a dairy for the supply of pure, wholesome, and unadulterated milk for the special use of invalid and delicate ladies and their infant children visiting the Park.... There is a cottage being erected, with a handsome steeple and ornamental turrets, for the accommodation of ladies and infants. There will be female attendants there, and all the regular conveniences. In the basement cows will be kept in readiness to supply the demand made of them. Around this cottage a fine area of land is set apart for a playground, exclusively for the very young children, being distinct and separate from the present boys' and girls' playground.

Cows, goats and poultry grazed and foraged on the lawn immediately to the building's south, and this fanciful, Victorian Gothic gingerbread concoction—redolent with the lowing of dairy cows and the earthy scent of the barnyard—must have delighted young visitors who knew nothing other than city life. The Dairy was constructed of Manhattan schist and grey granite and ornamented with Gothic windows recalling English country churches. An open loggia of polychrome wood mirrors the actual dairy building, its steeply pitched slate roof topped by a slender belfry inspired by the medieval church spires of Cologne, the austere volumetrics of which had so impressed Vaux and George Truefitt during their Continental tour of 1847. By the 1950s, an era of wanton official vandalism, the dilapidated loggia was razed. The Dairy itself was spared, doubtless only because its stone construction demanded too much effort to demolish, and it was ignominiously

Above: The legendary Casino stood near Fifth Avenue at 72nd Street and was built in 1864 after designs by Calvert Vaux as the Ladies' Refreshment Salon, a sedate restaurant serving unchaperoned women. In the Roaring Twenties, Mayor "Gentleman Jimmy" Walker ensured that the concession became an infamous nightclub and speakeasy, "the most beautiful and elegant restaurant in the world." In the Great Depression, Robert Moses ordered the building razed with Mayor Fiorello La Guardia's blessing.

Above: Facing financial difficulties, Vaux returned to work as a landscape architect for the city's Department of Public Parks at the end of his career, designing this unrealized project for a children's playhouse in 1891. Depicted is the building's east elevation, which would have straddled the 65th Street Transverse Road running beneath. Authors' watercolor.

converted to a storage shed. Its 1979 restoration remains one of the Conservancy's signal achievements, and the building has since served as the park's first visitor center.

The Sheepfold

The Sheepfold (*p. 201, top*), located on the northwest edge of Sheep Meadow near Central Park West at 66th Street, was built in 1871 after the designs of Mould, who had assumed Vaux's duties during the short-lived Tweed ring's ascendancy. Mould made the most of his moment in command and cancelled the Romanesque villa Vaux had designed for the Belvedere's terrace (*p. 83*), shifting funds to the grandiose Sheepfold, entirely his own initiative; with a budget of $70,000, it was among the park's most expensive buildings.

Exiled, Olmsted and Vaux ridiculed the structure from the sidelines: its scale, flamboyant polychromy and placement drew undue attention and disturbed the bucolic vistas from Sheep Meadow; it could only be reached by crossing West Drive on a blind curve, violating a cardinal rule of their design; it was a ridiculously expensive and overly pompous building for "its ostensible purpose...to provide a shelter, *at night* and in severe winter weather for the sheep used to keep down the grass on the adjoining Green." The coup de grâce, "its general aspect suggests a large English parochial school." Nonetheless, they judged the Sheepfold "handsome," and indeed the building is a lively admixture of textbook neo-Palladian massing—a recessed central pavilion and flanking end pavilions

linked by arcing galleries that trace an oval forecourt. A brilliant example of high Victorian Gothic polychromy, Mould's characteristically exuberant façade mixes banded red brickwork with crisply delineated detailing executed in blue stone, polished granite, gilded ironwork and Minton tiles, all sheltered beneath a steeply pitched, spirited roofscape clad in polychrome slate.

A flock of 200 Southdown sheep and their shepherd—a municipal employee—were housed on the splendid, albeit damp premises, with the end pavilions devoted to children's educational displays. For decades all went on with bucolic calm, the sheep crossing West Drive each morning to graze and returning each evening to the fold, until 1934 when, at the height of the Great Depression, Commissioner Moses, concerned that they would be poached for food, ordered the flock removed to Prospect Park, Brooklyn.

The building, which in 1912 the *Times* had already disparaged as "the unsightly old sheepfold which disfigures the west side of Central Park," was then leased as a restaurant, becoming the storied Tavern on the Green. Restaurant impresario Warner Le Roy, creator of the iconic Maxwell's Plum—which unleashed the scourge of quiche, Chardonnay, potted ferns, fairy lights and Tiffany lamps upon an unsuspecting generation—renovated the building as "a kind of living theater" in 1976, creating a sensation. Le Roy's flamboyant Willy Wonka wonderland—in its heyday the largest restaurant in America and the highest-grossing in Manhattan—closed in 2009, sensationally indebted. After a Conservancy-led restoration, the Parks Department let the Sheepfold to a new concessionaire in 2012, reviving the Tavern on the Green as a casual café offering takeout meals where once a pair of life-size wooden elk roamed beneath a Tiffany ceiling and a maharajah's chandelier.

Above: The Dairy, a neo-Gothic folly built in 1870 to offer fresh milk to city children, today houses the Conservancy's visitor center. Authors' watercolor.

Opposite, above: The flamboyant Sheepfold stands near Central Park West at 67th Street and was built in 1870 after the designs of Jacob Wrey Mould, seen here in a pre-construction rendering. Converted to the celebrated Tavern on the Green restaurant in 1934, the building was recently restored.

Opposite, below: The sheep that gave Sheep Meadow its name in a bucolic scene photographed in the late nineteenth century.

PARK MAP

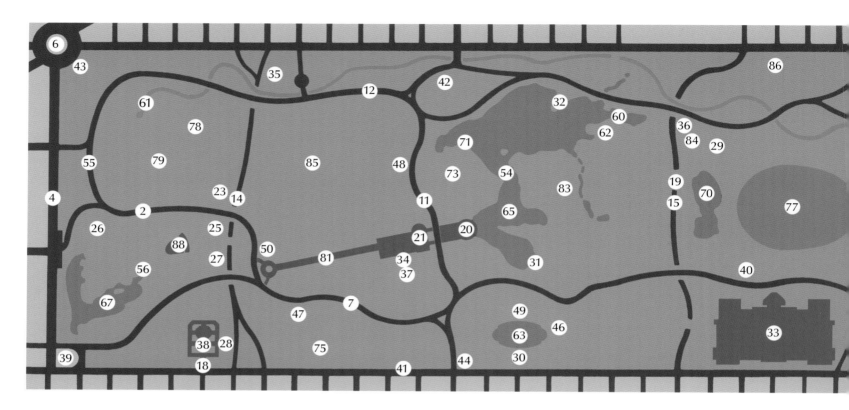

THE MAJOR LANDMARKS and topographical features of Central Park are listed below and keyed to this map, as well as features illustrated or cited in the main text. For clarity, a number of secondary structures, notably many bridges and sculptures, have been omitted.

Major Thoroughfares and Drives

1. Bridle Path
2. Center Drive
3. Central Park North
4. Central Park South
5. Central Park West
6. Columbus Circle
7. East Drive
8. Fifth Avenue
9. Frawley Circle
10. Frederick Douglass Circle
11. Terrace Drive
12. West Drive

13. West 85th Street
14. 65th Street Transverse Road
15. 79th Street Transverse Road
16. 86th Street Transverse Road
17. 97th Street Transverse Road

Buildings and Structures

18. The Arsenal
19. Belvedere Castle
20. Bethesda Fountain
21. Bethesda Terrace
22. The Blockhouse
23. The Carousel
24. Charles A. Dana Discovery Center
25. Chess and Checkers House
26. Cop Cot rustic log pavilion
27. The Dairy
28. Delacorte Musical Clock
29. Delacorte Theatre
30. Kerbs Boathouse
31. Loeb Boathouse
32. Ladies' Pavilion

33. Metropolitan Museum of Art
34. Naumburg Bandshell
35. Sheepfold
36. Swedish Cottage
37. Wisteria Pergola
38. Central Park Zoo

Memorials and Monuments

39. General Sherman Monument at Grand Army Plaza
40. The Obelisk
41. Richard Morris Hunt Memorial
42. Strawberry Fields
43. USS *Maine* Monument
44. Waldo Hutchins Bench
45. William T. Stead Memorial

Sculpture

46. *Alice in Wonderland*
47. *Balto*
48. *The Falconer*

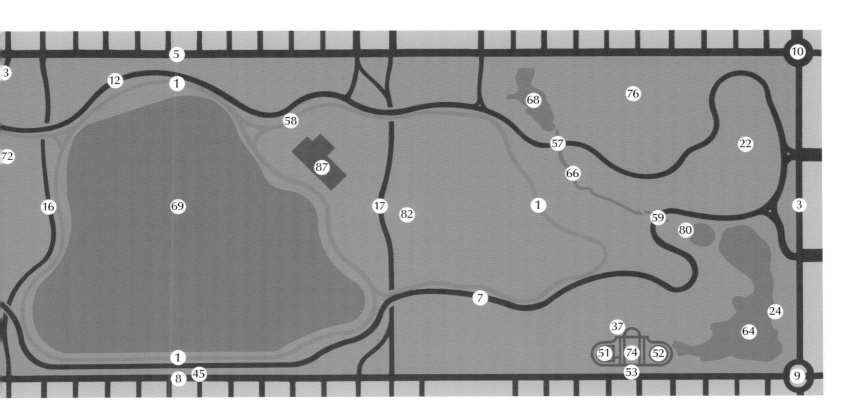

49. *Hans Christian Andersen*
50. *The Indian Hunter*
51. *The Secret Garden*
52. Untermyer Fountain
53. Vanderbilt Gate

Bridges and Arches

54. Bow Bridge
55. Dipway Arch
56. Gapstow Bridge
57. Glen Span Arch
58. Gothic Bridge
59. Huddlestone Arch
60. Oak Bridge at Bank Rock Bay
61. Pine Bank Arch
62. Ramble Arch

Lakes, Ponds and Meers

63. Conservatory Water
64. Harlem Meer
65. The Lake

66. The Loch
67. The Pond
68. The Pool
69. The Reservoir
70. Turtle Pond
71. Wagner Cove

Topographical Features, Gardens and Recreation

72. Arthur C. Ross Pinetum
73. Cherry Hill
74. Conservatory Garden
75. The Dene
76. Great Hill
77. Great Lawn
78. Heckscher Ball Fields
79. Heckscher Playground
80. Lasker Rink and Pool
81. The Mall
82. North Meadow Recreation Center
83. The Ramble
84. Shakespeare Garden

85. Sheep Meadow
86. Summit Rock
87. Tennis Courts
88. Wollman Rink

SELECTED BIBLIOGRAPHY

Alex, William, and Tatum, George B. *Calvert Vaux, Architect & Planner*. New York, 1994.

Alphand, Jean-Charles Adolphe. *Les promenades de Paris*. Paris, 1867–1873.

Baker, Paul. *Richard Morris Hunt*. Boston, 1986.

Beveridge, Charles E., Rocheleau, Paul, and Larkin, David. *Frederick Law Olmsted: Designing the American Landscape*. New York, 1998.

Burrows, Edwin G., and Wallace, Mike. *Gotham: A History of New York City to 1898*. New York, 1999.

Caro, Robert A. *The Power Broker: Robert Moses and the Fall of New York*. New York, 1975.

Cedar Miller, Sara. *Central Park, An American Masterpiece*. New York, 2003.

Cook, Clarence C. *A Description of the New York Central Park*. New York, 1869.

D'Alton, Martina. *The New York Obelisk*. New York, 1993.

Dixon, Roger, and Muthesius, Stefan. *Victorian Architecture*. London, 1978.

Downing, Andrew Jackson (Twombly, Robert, ed.). *Andrew Jackson Downing: Essential Texts*. New York, 2012.

_____. *Rural Essays*. New York, 1858.

_____. *Treatise on the Theory and Practice of Landscape Gardening*. New York, 1852.

Emerson, Ralph Waldo. *Nature*. Boston, 1836.

Frederick Law Olmsted Association, ed. *The Central Park*. New York, 1990.

Gorringe, Henry H. *Egyptian Obelisks*. New York, 1882.

Guild, W. H., Jr., and Perkins, Frederick B. *The Central Park: Photographed*. New York, 1864.

Heckscher, Morrison H. *Creating Central Park*. New York: The Metropolitan Museum of Art Bulletin, New Series, vol. 65, No. 3 (Winter 2008).

_____. *The Metropolitan Museum of Art: An Architectural History*. New York, 1995.

Howells, William Dean. *Impressions and Experiences*. New York, 1896.

Hunt, John Dixon. *Gardens and the Picturesque: Studies in the History of Landscape Gardening*. Cambridge, MA, 1992.

Hunt, John Dixon, and Willis, Peter. *The Genius of the Place: The English Landscape Garden 1620–1820*. London, 1975.

Hunt, Richard Morris. *Designs for the Gateways of the Southern Entrances to the Central Park*. New York, 1866.

Jones, Owen. *The Grammar of Ornament*. London, 1856.

_____. *Details and Ornament from the Alhambra*. London, 1845.

Kowsky, Francis R. *Country, Park & City: The Architecture and Life of Calvert Vaux*. New York, 1998.

Loudon, John Claudius. *An Encyclopædia of Gardening*. London, 1822.

Martin, Justin. *Genius of Place: The Life of Frederick Law Olmsted*. Cambridge, MA, 2011.

Mason, William. *The English Garden: A Poem*. London, 1772.

Moldenke, Charles E. *The New York Obelisk: Cleopatra's Needle*. New York, 1891.

Nevins, Allen, and Thomas, Milton, eds. *The Diary of George Templeton Strong: Young Man in New York, 1835–1849*. 4 vols. New York, 1952.

New York City Department of Parks and Recreation. "New York City Parks Department Annual Reports (with Central Park Annual Reports)." Available at: *http://www.nycgov-parks.org/news/reports/archive*.

Olmsted, Frederick Law. *Public Parks*. Brookline, MA, 1892.

_____. (MacLaughlin, Charles, and Beveridge, Charles, series eds.) *The Papers of Frederick Law Olmsted*. 7 vols. Baltimore, 1977–.

_____. *Walks and Talks of an American Farmer in England*. New York, 1858.

Olmsted, Frederick Law, Jr., and Kimball, Theodora, eds. *Frederick Law Olmsted, Landscape Architect, 1822–1903*. 2 vols. New York, 1922–1928.

Olmsted, Frederick Law, and Vaux, Calvert. *Description of a plan for the improvement of the Central Park. "Greensward."* New York, 1868 (1858).

Ossman, Laurie, Ewing, Heather, and Brooke, Steven. *Carrère & Hastings*. New York, 2011.

Parsons, Samuel, Jr. *Landscape Gardening*. New York, 1985.

_____. *Landscape Gardening Studies*. New York, 1910.

_____. *The Art of Landscape Architecture*. New York, 1915.

Reed, Henry Hope, and Duckworth, Sophia. *Central Park: A History and a Guide*. New York, 1967.

Reed, Henry Hope, McGee, R. M., and Mipaas, Esther. *Bridges of Central Park*. New York, 1990.

Repton, Humphry. *Sketches and Hints on Landscape Gardening*. London, 1794.

Rogers, Elizabeth Barlow. *Frederick Law Olmsted's New York*. New York, 1972.

_____. *Rebuilding Central Park: A Management and Restoration Plan*. Boston, 1987.

Roper, Laura Wood. *FLO: A Biography of Frederick Law Olmsted*. Baltimore, 1973.

Rosenzweig, Roy, with Blackmar, Elizabeth. *The Park and the People: A History of Central Park*. Ithaca, NY, 1992.

Rousseau, Jean-Jacques. *Julie, ou la nouvelle Héloïse*. Paris, 1761.

Ruskin, John. *Lectures on Landscape*. Oxford, 1871.

_____. *Modern Painters*. 5 vols. London, 1851–1860.

_____. *The Seven Lamps of Architecture*. London, 1849.

_____. *The Stones of Venice*. 3 vols. London, 1851–1853.

Rybczynski, Witold. *A Clearing in the Distance: Frederick Law Olmsted and America in the Nineteenth Century*. New York, 1999.

Spann, Edward K. *The New Metropolis: New York City 1840–1857*. New York, 1981.

Stokes, I. N. Phelps. *The Iconography of Manhattan Island, 1498–1990*. New York, 1918.

Trollope, Anthony. *North America*. London, 1862.

Truefitt, George. *Architectural Sketches on the Continent*. London, 1847.

Turner, Robert. *Capability Brown and the Eighteenth-century English Landscape*. New York, 1985.

Vaux, Calvert. *Villas and Cottages*. New York, 1857.

Voorsanger, Catherine Hoover, and Howat, John K. *Art and the Empire City: New York, 1825–1861*. New York, 2000.

Walpole, Horace. *A Description of the Villa of Horace Walpole*. Twickenham, 1774.

_____. *Essay on Modern Gardening*. Twickenham, 1780.

Whately, Thomas. *Observations on Modern Gardening*. London, 1770.

Wilson, Michael I. *William Kent: Architect, Designer, Painter, Gardener, 1685–1748*. London, 1984.

Wittemann, Adolph. *Central Park New York From Original Negatives by the Albertype Company*. New York, 1892.

ACKNOWLEDGMENTS AND PICTURE CREDITS

THIS BOOK BEGAN as the exhibition Central Park held at Didier Aaron, Inc. in October of 2003, which came to be through the counsel of Alan Salz, the gallery's director, and the encouragement of Hervé Aaron, its founder. Both have our enduring gratitude for their friendship and support. Nancy Druckman and Paula Beres of Didier Aaron have our warmest thanks for their many efforts on our behalf.

The initiative and encouragement of Charles Miers, our publisher, and David Morton, our editor, have made this volume a reality, and Douglas Curran has guided it smoothly through the editorial process. They have provided exceptional freedom for us to craft this book as we saw fit and expert guidance as the project evolved; authors are rarely so lucky to find themselves in such an ideal position, and we are extremely grateful for their support.

We thank the staffs of the New-York Historical Society, the Museum of the City of New York and the New York City Municipal Archives for their assistance when researching both our exhibition and this book. Morrison H. Heckscher generously guided us though the Metropolitan Museum of Art's holdings on Central Park while preparing our exhibition. We are grateful to Roberta Olson for the honor of having the watercolor illustrated on page 207 enter the New-York Historical Society's collections and for seeing it exhibited in the retrospective *Drawn by New York* in 2008 and 2009.

Finally, we warmly thank New Yorkers Philip San Filippo and Richard Cook for their long friendship and for their invaluable assistance over the course of this project.

We are deeply grateful to the talented group of photographers appearing below who have generously allowed us to reproduce their work. In particular we thank Cornelis Verwaal, who has provided a series of magnificent photographs, including several taken at our behest.

Illustrations not listed below are in the public domain and widely available.

2, 4, 6, 8, 11, 39, 43, 44, 47, 49, 51, 53, 55, 64, 65, 68, 69, 71, 73, 77, 79, 84–85, 88–89, 90–91, 93, 94, 98–99, 100–101, 108, 112, 114–115, 120–121, 126–127, 130, 131, 132, 133, 138, 139, 141, 143, 146, 148, 150, 151, 153, 157, 164, 165, 167, 168, 171, 177, 178–179, 185, 187, 188–189, 195, 199, 200, 202–203, 205, 207: Original watercolors ©2012 Edward Andrew Zega and Bernd H. Dams. http://architecturalwatercolors.com.

13, 62–63, 104–105, 107, 128, 152, 169: ©2009–2012 Cornelis Verwaal.

Cornelis Verwaal, a New York based photographer and former researcher/archivist at the Time Life Picture Collection, was born in the Netherlands and has privileged Central Park as a subject. http://cornelisverwaal.photoshelter.com.

14, 155: ©2012 Edward Yourdon.

Edward Yourdon is an internationally recognized information-technology consultant with a passion for photography. His work is widely published in leading media worldwide.

15, 46, 66–67, 87, 129: ©2011 Edward Andrew Zega.

16: ©2012 Mathew Knott.

Mathew Knott, a keen travel photographer for many years, enjoys the challenge of capturing the best perspectives of the places he visits.

17: ©2010 Joseph O. Holmes.

Joseph O. Holmes is a fine art photographer living and working in New York City. His work can be seen at http://streetnine.com.

18, 19, 22–23, 23, 33, 34 top and bottom, 37, 38, 40, 61, 124, 160, 162, 163, 175, 176, 181, 186, 201 bottom: The Library of Congress Prints & Photographs Online Catalog, available at http://www.loc.gov/pictures/.

20, 21: Courtesy the Frederick Law Olmsted National Historic Site.

26 bottom, 28, 31, 80–81, 125: Courtesy the Municipal Archives of the City of New York.

29: *Frederick Law Olmsted* by John Singer Sargent, used with kind permission from The Biltmore Company, Asheville, North Carolina.

58, 110: ©2012 Alfredo Bergna.

59: ©2012 Noel Y. Calingasan.

Noel Y. Calingasan is a neuroscientist by profession and a photography enthusiast. Born in the Philippines, he enjoys photographing New York City, where he currently lives.

70: ©2012 Elissa Shajia Haque.

72: ©2012 Gwen Williams.

Gwen Williams is a freelance photographer specializing in landscapes, cities and portraiture.

74: ©2008 John Groenendijk.

John Groenendijk is a Dutch freelance photographer of architecture, special events and nature. His work is published in the Netherlands and the U.S. http://www.flickr.com/people/fotograafjohn.

75: ©2011 Dana Hunting Photography, Seattle, WA. *Dana Hunting's fine art and travel photography is found at http://www.danahunting.com.*

76: George Bellows, *Fountain in Central Park*, courtesy the Hirshhorn Museum and Sculpture Garden, Smithsonian Institution, gift of Joseph H. Hirshhorn, 1966. Photography by Lee Stalsworth.

81 bottom, 83 top, 96, 201: Courtesy the Avery Architectural Library of Columbia University.

95: ©Sara Cedar Miller/Central Park Conservancy.

97: ©2012 Jake Rajs.

New Yorker Jake Rajs has published sixteen books, and his award-winning photographs have been featured in countless magazines, books and albums; his prints are in numerous museums and private collections. www.jakerajs.com.

108–109: ©2012 Fran Simó.

Fran Simó's photography has been exhibited internationally, and he has curated numerous exhibitions and books. He is president of Barcelona Photobloggers, cofounder of Caja Azul and member of the Calle 35 photography collective. http://fransimo.info.

113: ©2012 Phil Haber Photography LLC.

Phil Haber is a landscape and nature photographer based in the Hudson Valley, NY, and a contributor to Getty Images. His photos have been exhibited in the New York area and appear on numerous websites. His work may be found at http://philhaberphotography.com.

117: ©2012 Anne Canright.

Anne Canright is a writer and photographer who lives on California's Central Coast.

118: ©2012 Raymond Larose.

Raymond Larose is a freelance photographer based in New Hampshire whose work has appeared in local, national and international publications.

119: ©2012 John Blough.

John Blough is an amateur photographer who enjoys visiting and photographing all parts of New York City.

147: Courtesy the Cleveland Museum of Natural History.

150: Aerial perspective of the 1934 Central Park Zoo. Reproduced by permission of the Wildlife Conservation Society Archives, New York.

159: ©2012 Hasan Ahmed.

Hasan Ahmed's photography may be found at http://onlinepixels.com.

163, 166, 172: ©2012 Bernd H. Dams.

183: ©2012 Lissette Carrera.

INDEX

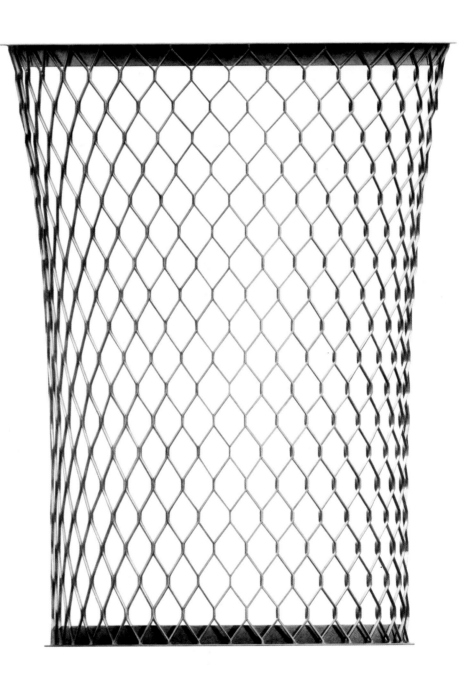

Right: An elevation of the iconic New York City trash basket, revealing its geometric elegance. Once ubiquitous, the containers are now reserved for the park precincts. Authors' watercolor.

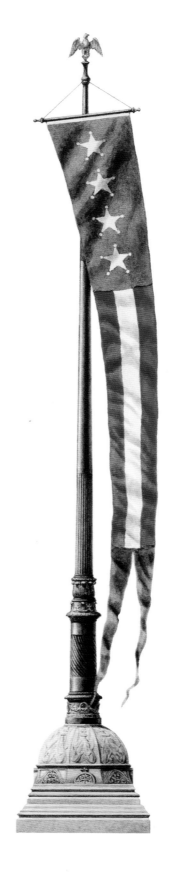

Right: One of a pair of gonfalons bracketing the lower esplanade fronting the Lake at Bethesda Terrace (Chapter III). Central Park was in large part constructed during the Civil War, thus explaining this early design for a patriotic banner. Authors' watercolor.